AF395000

Reflections and interpretations

– The Freedom Writers' teaching methodology

Torbjørn Ydegaard (Ed.)

Reflections and interpretations
– The Freedom Writers' teaching methodology

All the forces in the world are not as powerful as an idea whose time has come.

Victor Hugo

All sorrows can be borne if you put them into a story or tell a story about them

Isak Dinesen/Karen Blixen

Colophone

©Torbjørn Ydegaard and the contributors, 2015
Reflections and Interpretations – The Freedom Writers' methodology

Publisher: BoD – Books on Demand, Copenhagen, Denmark
Production: BoD – Books on Demand GmbH - Norderstedt, Germany

ISBN: 9788771702224

Content

Torbjørn Ydegaard

Foreword

For a long time I have considered to produce a book on The Freedom Writer–methods as I have felt a professional need for texts explaining, not only *how* the tools are being used, but also *why* they work so convincingly well. I was looking not for guidelines, but for explanations based on theory. Within some few hours, walking my dog in the forest, I realized the book should be an anthology written by the help of my fellow *Freedom Writer Teachers* – who else could do it as an *insider job*? I therefore wrote the following text on our Facebook-page. Now you are holding the result in your hands!

I know Erin is not too keen to talk about the theories behind the Freedom Writers methods, and as long as the methods give the desired results the pragmatism of 'practice' is of course well worth focusing on. However, as a college-teacher I often feel the need to be able to relate the practice to theories. Students writing about the methods in examination papers will be asked to refer them to theories – this is the conditions of 'academia', like it or not!

 Therefore, I need a book containing reflections and interpretations on the Freedom Writers teaching methodology!

 I cannot write such a book on my own. I need the help of my fellow Freedom Writer Teachers. If anyone of you would like to contribute to an anthology, it would be great. You can write a purely theoretical paper, or you can write with reference to your own practical experiences. I will write reflections based on readings of Hannah Arendt and Karl Popper – both philosophers of Jewish descent, with backgrounds in the German language-area and both had to flee the Nazi-regime. In addition, both with strong opinions on learning and teaching! There will be plenty of room for other perspectives, both the broad and well known and the more narrow views!

Conditions:

- *The target-groups will be primarily students of teaching on bachelor or diploma levels*
- *All texts will be in English*
- *There are no limits on the length of texts — short ones as well as long ones are welcome*
- *Deadline will be March 1. The book will then be presented at #5515*
- *The book will be published as print-on-demand, with an ISBN-number*
- *The book will be available on Amazon — and maybe other platforms*
- *All royalties from the book will be donated to The Freedom Writers Foundation*

The texts in this book are short and long, reflecting practical matters, giving specific suggestions, going into depth with theories of learning and teaching. But they are all written with the sole concern to bring education to those in need — and whom among us can honestly say they are not in need?

All texts are arranged in alphabetic order due to the author's surname.

Torbjørn Ydegaard

Erin Gruwell

To right a wrong with words, not weapons

Twenty years ago, when I walked into Room 203 at Woodrow Wilson High School in Long Beach, California, I had no idea that those same struggling students who sat before me would become the inspiration for an educational movement. A movement that transcended their simple classroom and their chaotic community to help validate vulnerable learners in other classrooms and other communities reach similar success.

I once described my students—the Freedom Writers—as colorful as a box of crayons…and as this educational journey has spread to other countries and continents, the crayons have multiplied and the colors have intensified. Now, other shades share their story and a variety of hues paint personal pictures. While the stories and pictures may be slightly different based on community, culture or class, there is a common thread throughout – a thread of hope that celebrates change and that empowers the human spirit to soar.

Since my initial lessons to write a wrong with words, not weapons, the Freedom Writers have turned their literary lessons into a legacy. One of the catalysts for their change was when Miep Gies, the simple secretary who helped hide Anne Frank in the attic, shared the importance of turning on "a small light in a dark room." Her moving metaphor motivated my students to become torchbearers. And although the Freedom Writers may have started this odyssey as struggling students, through time, they have transformed into talented teachers who help turn the darkness into light. Luckily, Miep Gies ignited their passion, and now, the Freedom Writers pass the torch to others. Each flame that they light becomes a "Freedom Writer Teacher" and collectively, their fire burns brightly.

The Freedom Writers and I wanted to share the magic we experienced during our educational journey, and to do so, "The Freedom Writers Diary" became a testament to our time in Room 203 and beyond. Once our book made its way into the hands of teachers and students alike, we decided it was time to try and capture lightening in a bottle (or better yet, a book) and publish a teacher's guide that would showcase strategies and the creative curriculum that defined my pedagogical process. And thus, the Freedom Writer Teacher movement was born. We are now 400 strong. And growing. The Freedom Writer Teachers geographical reach spans states in America, provinces in Canada, and over a dozen countries worldwide, but our purpose is palpable—to give a voice to the voiceless.

In the spirit of giving a voice to the voiceless, we discovered that teachers' voices need to be heard too because they are story tellers themselves. To celebrate their unique story, along with those they serve, we invite these dynamic educators to Long Beach to spend a week with the original Freedom Writers and me to participate in an intensive, professional development training designed to improve their professional practice. While the Freedom Writer Teachers are with us, each of them get a sneak-peak at the actual ingredients used to create our "secret sauce." Our intention is that after enculturation in the Freedom Writers ethos and methodology, each of the Freedom Writer Teachers will return to their own educational environment with a purpose. Upon return, our goal is for them to take the recipe for the "secret sauce" and make it their own. We encourage Freedom Writer Teachers to adapt, tweak and personalize the lesson plans from Room 203 into their own setting, for their own students. May they add a personal touch or a modern day twist, may they do it better than we did, and may they continue to share their success.

Thus, the success of the Freedom Writer Teachers is that they collaborate, commiserate and celebrate with one another. Freedom Writer Teachers are bold thinkers, they take risks and they solve problems. They are resilient in the face of bureaucracy, they are relevant when challenged with unrealistic expectations, and they fight to create a healthy sense of self. And not only do they revel in relationships, but they foster familial bonds. Like my father once told me, they too are "blessed with a burden"—and that burden is to reach their brethren, to overcome obstacles, to tell their tale, and to dare to dream.

While using the Freedom Writers curriculum in their respective classrooms, eight passionate educators decided to showcase the pedagogical and instructional practices that they use to engage, enlighten and empower. The eight collaborators of this book may speak different languages, practice different customs, and teach different students, but they each share a universal belief—that the art of teaching is bigger than all of us. These noble teachers help inspire many voices, be it that of a troubled teen, an aspiring college student, or even a soldier on the heels of healing. I am proud of how this compelling compilation weaves best practices together, gives credibility to an educational movement, and encourages the teacher in each of us. Whether you stand at a pulpit, a podium or in front of a room full of pupils, may you, like these phenomenal Freedom Writer Teachers, teach one to teach another!

Erin Gruwell

Doug Ball

Freedom Writers Pedagogy: Literacy, Hip-Hop & Hope

*For the first time I heard a teacher
take a question seriously.*
– Freedom Writers Diary, #40

Apologia

Given their chances of dropping out or being gunned down in the streets what happened to the students in room 203, Wilson High, was an educational miracle. A white, middle-class teacher from a gated community discovered in the *weltanschauung* of her street-smart students their "terms" for becoming school-smart. *The Freedom Writers Diary* (1997) and *The Freedom Writers Diary Teacher's Guide* (2007) reveal their pedagogy of hip-hop and hope, whereby teacher became renegade, gangstas became grad students. In Part I of this paper I discuss why Freedom Writer pedagogy (FWP) is a relevant model for teacher education acquainting pre-service teachers with the critical issues and choices they will face in today's diverse classrooms, especially when it comes to equal education opportunity for students put at risk by poverty and despair; by institutionalized racism and oppression. Academics may dismiss FWP as cultish California cumbaya because it lacks roots in theory and researched-based practices; however, I connect its well documented, undeniably wholesome outcomes to Freire's theory of critical pedagogy as well as to academic studies about the needs of at-risk students (e.g., Murray & Naranjo, 2011). In Part II of this paper I discuss in particular how a curriculum of relevant literacy awakened the Freedom Writers' critical questions, critical hope, and *conscientização*, which Freire, the Brazilian liberation theologian, considered requisite for emancipatory education.

Part I

"Hands up, don't shoot…"
In 1989 Aarons predicted the greatest challenge facing educators in the next 20 years will be helping the underclass of poor students. Now in 2015 with nearly 25% of children in the USA living in poverty[1], the recalcitrant achievement gap is still the pachyderm in the classroom. In too many urban schools dropout rates[2] are as high as 40% and when 98% of students in these schools are Latinos and/or African Americans (often the case), the equal education victory of Brown *v.* Board has become perversely distorted.

Shorris (1998) described the anomie of oppressive forces that surround the poor, including racism and police brutality, creating a state of perpetual panic, powerlessness, and hopelessness. Recent studies show chronic stressors associated with growing up in poverty have deleterious effects on a child's cog-

---

[1] According to National Center for Educational Statistics, 47.55% of students in the US. are eligible for Free and Reduced Lunch (FRL). In Washington, DC schools, 72.3% receive FRL, and in a nearby elementary school in Arlington County, Virginia, one of the most affluent school districts in the US, 80% of students are recipients.

[2] NB: dropout rates are typically based on "failure to graduate on-time" statistics.

nitive development, if not their life expectancy (Stein, 2009). Endemic factors that put students at risk have been well documented by noted authors (e.g., Kozol, 2005), in academic studies (e.g., Murray & Naranjo, 2008), and in recent headlines (e.g., "Black & Brown Lives Matter"). Barr & Parret (2001) identified three factors present by third grade that predict within 90-95% accuracy a student will eventually drop out,

- Having been retained
- Attending school with other poor children
- Reading below grade level

What chances, if any, would a vulnerable child have of beating such grim odds?

How do they play the inequity cards they've been dealt? – growing up in a community of poverty, drugs, gangs, police brutality; being undocumented, raised by single parent, in foster care, the projects, or homeless? A victim of domestic abuse, sexual abuse, bullying, illiteracy, and hopelessness? Attending school where they face racism, low or no expectations, pernicious labels, stereotypes, and draconian discipline practices?

At-risk youth arrive at school far from ready to learn, and public school programs tend to isolate them, stigmatize them, and place them in programs that widen the academic gap....school policies and practices that intellectually and psychologically brutalize *[at-risk] students are rooted in educational mythology that has endured for decades in spite of mounting evidence to the contrary.*

(Barr & Parret, 2001, p.34, italics added)

How does a vulnerable child overcome the accumulated anomie of society, streets, and school and not end up a drop-out, thug, addicted, drive-by casualty, victim, incarcerated?

What are the chances we can we prepare teachers to meet what Aarons (1989) had presaged to be the greatest challenge facing us in the 21st century? For what W.E.B. Du Bois saw as the most fundamental civil right?

> *Of all the civil rights for which the world has struggled and fought for 5,000 years, the right to learn is undoubtedly the most fundamental.*
>
> (Du Bois, 1949)

And for what Dewey believed we owe all children in our society?

> *What the best and wisest parent wants for [their] own child that must we want for* all *the children of the community. Any other ideal is narrow and unlovely, and acted upon,* it destroys our democracy.
>
> (Dewey, 1907, p.19, italics added)

"I teach because I search, because I question...." (Freire, 1998, p. 35).

My younger brother, a high school dropout, was incarcerated at age 18 for dealing hard drugs on the streets of Washington, DC. He himself was a heroin addict. In a letter he wrote me from federal prison, circa 1970, he said what he'd learned "up the river" had freed him. For years after his release until he finished his master's degree in counseling at Lincoln University, he joked he'd earned his college degree in prison. He'd already earned a Ph.D. from the streets.

Before I earned my Ph.D. and prior to becoming a professor of teacher education, I taught special education in upper elementary and middle schools. With only a "degree of caring," I'd actually started my teaching career as a literacy volunteer tutoring basic reading skills to inmates in a correctional work camp. Their path to prison seemed inevitable given the anomie in their lives. Most were Black, in their early twenties, from poor inner cities. None believed they could be taught how to read. One of my students who'd failed to read in school (but had learned to drive by stealing a Fleetwood), dictated this school memory:

> *I remember when I was back in school it was fun to me. Even to this day I know that I was hangin' with the wrong people but it seemed like everyone was learning but me. I like most all the teacher. All try their best to help me. When I got put out of school it really hurt me…. My mother really try to keep or should I said wanted us to finish school because she didn't have the time to go to school.…I left home at age 12…*
>
> – "Mike's Journal" 7/22/86 [3]

I became a public school teacher because I wanted to see firsthand the reasons why students like Mike fail to learn to read in school. In racist towns I taught kids from the wrong side of

---

[3] "Mike's Journal" appeared in *Reading, Writing, Route 29*, a collection of language experiences stories privately published in 1988 with a grant from Sidney Sheldon by Literacy Volunteers of Fauquier County (VA) for local distribution.

the tracks, in Appalachia I taught students who'd rather be coonhuntin' than struggling to pass state-mandated literacy tests. In schools where I taught it was not uncommon for a teacher to point to a certain troubled student and declare in a whisper, sometimes cynically, sometimes with a burden of care, "We know where he'll end up."

How educators can avoid resignation to myopic prognoses for at-risk students became the central question of my doctoral dissertation (Ball, 1999). Subsequently in education courses I've tried to help pre-service teachers develop the skills, dispositions, and self-efficacy to teach *all* students and especially to believe they can help prevent, or at least mitigate, the inevitable fates of students who are at high risk.

My most astute friend, an attorney, once remarked that anyone who believes in equal education opportunity is pathological. He may have a point, given dropout rates, the byzantine politics of reform, and the mindset of many educators. A syllogism I've often read (e.g., Kerr, 2012) or that I heard in the teachers' lounge, and have heard from more than a few pre-service teachers goes, "If those students and their families don't care about education, why should I care to teach them?"

> *...if teachers are to educate* all *children,...they must receive training and preparation for dealing with issues that children [from at-risk] environments bring to school with them.*
>
> (Edwards et al., 1999, p. xxiv)

Maybe I *am* pathological but I've searched for engaging and transformative ways to get my message across believing the culture of teaching and education that puts at-risk students further at risk needs to change. Many of my mostly white, middle-class female students have never had intensive, extensive interactions with people who are different than themselves, ethnically, culturally, socio-economically. How do teacher educators prepare students to consider what's at stake in diverse classrooms? To see the inequities in schools and society that allow educational inequality. Moreover to resist seeing only their circumstantial pathologies and instead *choose* to look for the potential in street-smart kids, the ones with Ph. D.s from the streets. Lisa, a Freedom Writer Teacher[4], posted on our Moodle site,

> *Teaching is a paradox. Our inner-most self is made public. Who we are at the core is on the line each day, which makes for a most destructive or most creative environment, or a complacent or extraordinary [one]....What is it that makes us choose?*

What is it that makes us choose? Essentially this is what I want my students to consider. The daily choice teachers face: to be destructive and complacent or creative and extraordinary, especially when it comes to being purveyors of equal education opportunity.

If problems of at-risk youth are complex so are the solutions (Pianta & Walsh, 1996).
I realized when I taught basic literacy to middle school students who came from the wrong side of the tracks and who'd fallen

---

[4] The Freedom Writer Foundation recruits teachers internationally to participate in professional development workshops where they experience Freedom Writers pedagogical methods. Currently there are 400 Freedom Writer Teachers.

through the cracks that at-risk students, like rare hothouse plants, require just the right conditions in order to thrive. Conditions they can't provide for themselves (Ball,1999). The challenges I faced, dealing with their resistance and inherent distrust of me their "honky" teacher, creating age-appropriate materials and learning activities, advocating for them, especially the daily struggle to keep them out of in-school suspension, was nothing compare to the challenge of helping them develop their capacity to struggle to become independent readers. (cf. Malcolm X's "A Homemade Education.")

Given the complex needs of so-called at-risk students and the statistical chances of their thriving in school and in the world, they require a radically sensitive and equally critical pedagogy. Again, they need teachers who can see potential rather than pathologies (Murray & Zvoch, 2011). A far cry from a pedagogy of one-size-fits-all, teaching-to-the-test or a core curriculum. Which theory, sanctioned evidence-based way of knowing could prove within acceptable margins of statistical errors that certain pedagogical practices can transform a gangsta into a grad student?

"….there is no such thing as teaching without research and research without teaching…" (Freire, 1998, p. 35).
In the Freedom Writers' pedagogy (FWP) I see a relevant and revelatory model for teacher education, which happens to reflect multiple best practices in the published research about teaching at-risk students[5], but in and of itself is not the direct result of

---

5 FWP (See "Ms. G's Secret Sauce, p. 5, 2007) resonates with a host of published research findings about meeting the educational needs of at-risk stu-

educational theory or research-based practices. FWP hardly developed from theory-to or research-to-practice. As far as I can tell it evolved from a different path. Similarly one of my most entrenched beliefs about educating *all* students doesn't come from educational theory or research, but from a 1950s abstract expressionist who wrote about his paint splattered canvases, "teknic is the result of a need." FWP evolved as a pedagogy of need. Given our predominate culture of data-driven decision-making, this may be construed as both pathological and heretical. Richard LaVoie is well-known for this comment about what fairness means in a classroom of diverse learners, "Fairness does not mean everyone gets the same. Fairness means everyone gets what they *need*" (Rosen, 1989).

"Hope is an ontological need" (Freire, 1994, p.8).
In 2003 when I'd first read *The Freedom Writers Diary* (1997), and then heard Erin Gruwell speak at Salisbury University as part of a distinguished scholar lecture series, it struck me like a lightening bolt that what had occurred in their classroom was the kind of educational reform needed to occur so no child is left behind or left out. In particular the Freedom Writers' transformation through "critical" literacy[6] reminded me of Freire's revolutionary dictum (1989) – to read the word those who historically have been denied education must learn to read their world. To see

---

dents including, forming trusting relations with teachers, looping, authentic literacy activities, providing students choice and voice; teachers holding high expectations, asking higher-order questions; student engagement through cooperative learning, multicultural content, building classroom community, bibliotherapy, relevant/meaningful/purposeful curriculum, etc., etc., etc.

[6] The evolving definition of critical pedagogy is discussed in Nolen (2011).

themselves as learners those who've been denied educational opportunity need to develop what Freire called *conscientização*[7], that is, to see themselves within the socio/cultural historical context of their oppression. Freire wrote, "Liberation is a praxis: the action and reflection of men and women upon their world in order to transform it" (2000, p. 60). As Maya Angelou realized, "Segregation shaped me. Education liberated me" (in Gates, 2009, p. 29). The Freedom Writers were similarly freed. Reading the word and the world transformed them, then they wrote about their lives, and that changed their world.

What had also struck me about Erin Gruwell's 2003 talk at Salisbury University to a jam-packed auditorium was how the audience of students connected with her.[8] Here is an excerpt from a recollection I wrote about that night,

In the past we'd had such notable speakers as Herbert Kohl, Alfie Kohn, Linda Darling-Hammond, Jonathan Kozol, Cornel West, Luis Garden Acosta, and Nel Noddings. These are accomplished outspoken scholars/activists in the field of educational reform. Each has contributed something to the cause of equal education. Yet as brilliant as they are, more often than not, when they spoke to the young college audience (required to attend the lecture) rarely did they connect with them. Some spoke way over their heads so students weren't engaged, and many headed for the exits prematurely. Few if any would ever attend the post-lecture reception. Then that fall you

---

[7] *Conscientização* in English, conscientization. I prefer to use the latter because as with many Portuguese words it is difficult to fully translate.

[8] Similarly students in my teacher education courses connect with *The Freedom Writers Diary*. It's the only text I assign that engages them and they will read cover-to-cover. I discuss their uncanny connections and reflections about it in "Postcards to Freedom Writers" (Ball (2015).

came and spoke. That night the students listened, they stayed. There was no mass exit that night. They lined up to meet you, the line stretched across the reception room and all the way down the long lobby. I'd never seen our education students so alive or inspired, in or out of the classroom. They connected with you and your students' story. We were never the same...

Erin Gruwell's was the most successful, memorable lecture in that series. And she delivered her talk without podium or PowerPoint. And as I recall without statistics, rhetoric, histrionics, or theory. She just told a story.

Freedom Writers Diary – a Textbook for Diversity or Cumbaya....?

Critics of the Freedom Writers phenomenon may dismiss Erin Gruwell as another white missionary teacher saving the ghetto kids, just another Hollywood cliché. In a recent edition of the bestselling text book I've used for the past 15 years in my teacher education courses, this statement warns pre-service teachers about miracles in the classroom:

One limitation of all teachers is that they cannot accomplish the miracles portrayed in the popular media, even if they are very good at what they do (Moore, 2007). Real teachers can't be perky, self-sacrificing, idealistic, and influential as those shown in films....
(p. 38, Hallahan, Kauffman, & Pullen, 2011).

Though I'm aware there's no place for magical thinking in Freire's liberation pedagogy[9], I still bristle at the rationale and assumptions of wet-blanket statements about miracles in the education of students who are hard to reach and teach. I don't know how else to describe what happened in Room 203 where students deemed least likely to thrive not only graduated and many earned college degrees (some now earning their Ph.D.s) but who also wrote a book that was to become an international bestseller. Granted replicating this phenomenon may be setting the bar a tad high for most teachers but preparing them to raise expectations for students considered uneducable is hardly unorthodox. Moreover to eschew idealism and self-sacrifice in teaching repudiates what's at the core of liberal arts education does it not? Such moral qualities are apparent in philosophical beliefs espoused in the liberal arts canon, from Socrates to Dr. Suess. Why else would we have students read Mill's *On Liberty* or MLK's "Letter from a Birmingham Jail"? Doing the right thing rarely means sticking with the status quo.

"The freedom to learn...has been bought by bitter sacrifice" (Dubois in Foner, 1970, p. 230).
Every day "ordinary" teachers do sacrifice to save students who are struggling to stay in school or who are on the brink of giving up. *Teaching Hope, Stories from the Freedom Writer Teachers* (2009) written by 150 teachers from all over the USA contains 150 stories about the sacrifice and idealism it takes. The Freedom Writ-

---

[9] "In order for the oppressed to unite they must first cut the umbilical cord of magic and myth that binds them to the world of oppression." (Freire, 2000, p. 156).

er Teachers teach in public schools, special education, correctional facilities, juvenile halls, alternative schools, elementary and secondary schools, universities, on Native American reservations, in big cities and remote towns. Our stories are diverse. The students we wrote about are diverse as are their problems: the 2nd grader who can't stay awake in class, the teen suicide, the student with HIV, the student who brings a knife to school, the student who can't read. In the foreword Anna Quindlen wrote,

> *...it's the teachers' turn to give the rest of us a window into....the real rhythms of a good teacher's life,* not bounded by June and September, or 8 and 3, but boundless because of the boundless needs of young people today *and the   dedication of those who work with them.*
>
> (2009, p.xii)

Even U.S. Secretary of Education, Arne Duncan, touts the necessity of sacrifice. To curb the recalcitrant dropout problem, Duncan said[10] it takes teachers who are committed beyond 9-3 school hours to making a difference in the lives of students – students who desperately need an adult's trust and mentoring (cf. Murray & Naranjo, 2008).

Sarason (1996) believed teachers are the number one agents of change. To stand up and advocate for vulnerable students' needs and rights often becomes tantamount to being a demagogue. And to effect change any revolutionary from Christ to Che would say ya gotta leave your comfort zone. And never look back.

---

[10] Duncan made this observation during a speech, which I heard broadcast live on C-Span Radio.

Teaching, learning, and doing-the-right-thing requires risk-taking. Even theory-to- practice requires leaps of faith. Granted we don't go about preparing teachers to be revolutionaries with Marxist banners or miracle workers with magic wands, angel wings, and halos. But do we have an option when it comes to helping them develop the capacity to recognize and do what is fair and just in the classroom? Admittedly that does takes a degree of saintly chutzpah. After all, "When you expect fair play, you create an infectious bubble of madness around you" (Holzer, 1992).

Ms G's Secret Sauce…

In *The Freedom Writers Diary Teacher's Guide* Erin Gruwell[11] included "leaving your comfort zone" as one of 12 main ingredients of FWP, aka "Ms G's Secret Sauce" (2008, p. 5). The teacher's guide contains community-building, diversity-awareness, self-appreciation, and getting-to-know-you activities that all necessitate leaving one's comfort zones.[12] Like any good simulation, these simple activities are powerful metaphors with endless potential for shared social-learning, especially about diversity, tolerance, respect, acceptance, and collaboration. In room 203 they were stepping stones toward engaging, enlightening, and empowering the Freedom Writers. In another paper (Ball, 2015)

---

[11] The Freedom Writers call her "Ms. G"

[12] These activities were developed in room 203 by Erin Gruwell and her students and have become the mainstay of their Freedom Writer Teacher Institute trainings where leaving one's comfort zone is essential. As one Institute participating teacher proclaimed, "I'm falling apart like a K-Mart lawn chair." The teacher guide provides lesson plans for these activities with step-by-step directions as well as annotations about their relevance and purpose.

I discuss how I've used Freedom Writer activities to temper pre-service teachers' dispositions and expand their pedagogical skills and beliefs.

In the next section of this paper I discuss how I have used several critical awakenings chronicled in the various incarnations of the Freedom Writers story (book, major motion picture, television news story, documentary film) to lead my teacher education students' to consider what's at stake when you expect equal education opportunity for at-risk students.

Part II

"…the premier demand upon all education is that Auschwitz not happen again."

– Adorno (in Nolen, p. 2011)

The Teacher in a Pearl Necklace…

One semester I had two students of color, Mara, a Latina from the South Bronx; and Audra, a single mother from Washington, DC, who got pretty upset when I showed the "Freedom Writer" PrimeTime Live! segment (Chung *et al.*,1998) and clips from the movie, *Freedom Writers* (LaGraveness, 2007). Audra started their vociferous protest,

> *"Why do they always show us the white teachers saving poor Black and Latino kids? There are teachers of color who do the same thing, why don't you ever show them?"*

Then Mara raised the stakes,

25

In response, I tried to point out to Mara and Audra that Erin Gruwell didn't "save" her students without their consent. It wasn't a one-sided process. No one can force "ghetto kids" to learn or change. By nature they gotta choose to do so. On their own terms. To become their teacher Erin had to learn from them what their terms were.

The salvation of the Freedom Writers was a reciprocal process that involved a teacher doing *with* her students, rather than doing *to* them. Freire called this communion, democratic education (2000).

But Audra and Mara still weren't buying it. The clash continued. Through anger and tears, the only color they could see was white privilege.

And I? Frankly I was dumbfounded by their reactions. In the years of using *Freedom Writers Diary* and showing these clips in my teacher education courses, I'd never heard similar protests. My students were usually inspired. As they watched the film footage they wept, but not because they felt the sting of white privilege.

From Mara and Audra I'd learned a lesson about teaching diversity. A cakewalk it's not. Tension comes with the territory when people speak, think, live, dress, eat, pray, learn and earn differently. If I was going to hold Ms G and the Freedom Writers phenomenon up as a model of hope for equal education opportunity, I needed to be prepared to engage in tougher dialogues.

"I teach because …. I submit myself to questioning..". (Freire, 1998, p. 35).
I couldn't answer Mara and Audra questions because frankly I didn't know how. Maybe such clashes are the highest form of teachable moments, when students' hard questions unmask the teacher's unsettling doubts, fears, and questions. That awkward inevitable moment when teacher and students realize the former isn't made of Teflon and doesn't have all the answers. Or that the professor is really a snake oil salesman producing special effects with smoke machines and mirrors. So I'm indebted to them. Their protests and tears made me question how I was teaching diversity, challenge my assumptions about the Freedom Writers phenomenon, made me reflect, and search for answers.

Yes, there are many unrecognized teachers of color – black, brown, and white, who make big differences every day, who deserve recognition, and some who do get it. I decided in the future when I did my lesson on at-risk students and Ms. G, I'd be sure to bring to class my copies of *Lives on the Boundaries*, by Mike Rose (2005) and *I Chose to Stay: A Black Teacher Refuses to Desert the Inner City* by Salome Thomas-El (2003).

I also considered *a posteriori* how my immediate response could've been in the form of a Socratic question. Afterwards I'd asked myself, "Does the color of a teacher's skin make any difference?" But I continued to struggle to the point of anguish with Mara and Audra's outcries. Until I read this,

> *….in the mid-1990's, teacher Erin Gruwell completely transformed the lives of 150 at-risk youths from Long Beach, California, by believing in them, opening up the world of literature for them and giving them a safe haven to express themselves through journaling. She*

stayed with the same students throughout all four years of high school, and every single one of them graduated....

Should we look scornfully upon her because she's white and her students were predominantly African-American, Hispanic and Asian? Many did when the fictionalized movie about her came out with Hilary Swank as Erin. Why? Because she's white? ....The woman took her considerable talents and her gigantic heart, and she worked her ass off to literally save a group of kids who worried about being killed every time they left home — some of them even in their homes. There are plenty of African-Americans who are changing lives and making a difference every day......[the author discusses Oprah's moral and philanthropic largesse.]

It was this passage especially that helped resolve my quandary,

I'm not African-American so I recognize there may be other sensitivities of which I'm not aware. I am Jewish, though, and I can tell you that I am grateful beyond words when Oskar Schindler saves a thousand Jews in Schindler's List — *even though he's German.* You can make a million Holocaust movies, real or fictionalized, and I'll appreciate every time a German helps a Jew....
The point is we need to help each other, and we need to keep encouraging people to do so. Dismissing someone's efforts is too easy — "oh, she's rich," "well, he has the connections" — is unfair and counterproductive....

(Mark, 2011, italics added)

I'll always be grateful to Mara and Audra for what I learned because they questioned me. If you're in a Nazi concentration camp, who cares what color your liberator's hair, eyes, tattoos, religious beliefs, or skin are? Teaching hope, freedom, and diversity are certainly not about knowing all the answers, but involve the willingness to engage in the tough dialogue it requires. Freire, the Brazilian liberation theologian, wrote in *Pedagogy of the Oppressed* (2000):

> *Dialogue …[presupposed by] humility, hope, faith and mutual trust…can only happen when we accept that others are different and can teach us something we   do not already know.*
>
> (p. 92)

This is one of two reasons I've always shown my teacher education students a particular scene in *Freedom Writers*, the movie (LaGravenese, 2007).

"Close your workbooks…"

The students in Room 203 are supposed to be doing meaningless activities in their grammar workbooks when Ms. G (played by Hillary Swank) intercepts a demeaning drawing being passed around her English class. They were snickering at the crudely drawn caricature of their Black classmate, "Jamal", which exaggerates his racial/facial features. This crude drawing that precipitated the transformation of the surly, disrespectful students in room 203, is reproduced in the *Freedom Writers Diary* (1998) and in close-up in the PrimeTime Live! documentary (Chung *et al.*,1998). In the Hollywood movie (LaGravenese, 2007) the scene goes like this –

Grabbing the drawing and holding it up, Ms G launches into a blistering tirade.

Ms. G: *You think this is funny? …Tito, would this be funny if it were a picture of you?*
Tito: *It's ain't me.*

She's tells them pointblank what the drawing reminds her of: Nazi propaganda that similarly caricatured, dehumanized and scapegoated Jews during the Holocaust. Compared to "the most famous gang in history" Ms. G belittles their Southern California gang mentality. Cambodians vs. Latinos vs. Black vs. Whites. Versus teacher.

Ms G: *You think you know all about gangs? You're amateurs….*

She then explains how Nazis saw Jews and Blacks as animals, their lives didn't matter, and life would be a whole lot better if they were all dead.

Ms G: *That's how a Holocaust happens and that's what you think of each other.…And it starts with a drawing like this….*

Then a very *very* tough dialogue erupts in the classroom in full-blown confrontation between white teacher and "ghetto kids", who see her as nothing more than a babysitter. Eva and Marcus are the most outspoken, the most vitriolic in their diatribes.

Marcus: *You don't know nothing about us, home girl!*

Ms G: *No, I don't know, Marcus, so why don't you explain it to me!?*

Marcus: *I ain't explaining shit to you!*

Eva speaks up to do some explaining and to deliver a few powerful punches.

Eva: *You don't know the pain we feel. You don't know what we gotta do. You got no respect for how we live…What are you doing in here that makes a goddamn difference in my life….?*

Ms G: *You don't feel respected, Eva? …to get respect you have to give it.*

André: *That's bullshit. Why should I give my respect to you?...I don't know you. How do I know you're not a liar….just because you're called a teacher.*

Eva: *White people always wanting their respect like they deserve it for free….*

Ms G: *I'm a teacher it doesn't matter what color I am.*

Eva: *It's all about color….So I hate white people on sight.*

Ms G: *You hate me?…you don't know me.*

Eva: *I know what you can do.*

The scene climaxes when Ms G unleashes her most incriminating salvo, after Marcus has defended the gang credo, *"we ain't afraid to die protecting our own…at least when you die for you own you die with respect."*

> Ms G: *So when you're dead you'll get respect? Is that what you think? ....You know what's going to happen when you die?.....do you think it's going to matter whether you were an original gangster? .....Nobody, nobody is going to want to remember you because all you left behind in this world is this! [Holds up the drawing of "Jamal"]*

There's dead silence in the classroom. Then. Close-up on Tito slowing raising his hand.

> Ms G: *[in disbelief] You're raising your hand?!*
> Tito: *That thing you said before, the holocaust?*
> Ms G: *The Holocaust... yes?*
> Tito: *What is it ?*
> Ms G: *[taken aback] Raise your hand if you know what the Holocaust is.*

Reverse shot of classroom, close-up of the sole white student who sheepishly raises a limp hand. His is the only raised hand. Ms G is speechless.

> Erin: *Raise your hand if anyone in this classroom has been shot at?*

All *but* the one white student raise their hands. The bell rings. The class exits *en masse*.

Ms G is left alone in the empty classroom, stunned. The audience is left on the edge of their seats[13].

---

[13] *Entre le Murs"*, a 2005 *cinema verite* film, also based on a book, is about a teacher in a Parisian suburban school where his students are mostly immigrants from Arabic countries. The clashes involving diversity in this film are

I'm the guy in the movie who asked that question...

In summer of 2012 I attended a Freedom Writers Teacher Institute (my third) in Long Beach, CA. During the Salsa party, a staple Institute event, I met the Freedom Writer who drew the picture of Sharaud ("Jamal"). I also met Carlos. He told me, *"I'm the guy in the movie who asked Ms G about the Holocaust."*

It'd been fifteen years since he'd asked Ms G his question. Carlos hands me his business card. He owns his own business. His two daughters flanked his legs. His ten year old with a prodigious voice had just sung Adele's, *"Rolling in the Deep"*, a capella; his other prodigy is in her soccer uniform. Carlos is her team's coach. His shiny tricked-out VW Jetta is parked within view. The last thing he says to me, in a humble way,

> *"Dr. Fresh, tell your college students it's me who asked that question, what's the holocaust."*

I was more than honored to meet Carlos and it has been an honor to tell my students about him and his question. To me it was his question that really began the transformation of both Ms G and his classmates. Freire wrote,

> *... teaching today consists in giving answers and not asking questions. It's what I call the "castration of curiosity"....the educator, generally, produces answers without having been asked anything!....*so what teachers ought to teach...should be supremely how to ask questions.... Because knowledge be-

---

equally unsettling as in Freedom Writers, and especially relevant in the wake of the culturally tensions that led to "Charlie Hebdo" and the Kosher Market murders.

gins with asking questions….[and] the only way to teach is by learning…*Perhaps this should be the first point …. in a training course for young people preparing to be teachers:* what does it mean to ask questions?…. *not to turn [it] into an intellectual game, but to experience the force of the question, experience the challenge it offers, …experience the curiosity and demonstrate it to students…one of the starting points in the training of educators in a liberating democratic approach would be this* apparently simple thing: *asking what it means to ask questions….*

(Freire, 2000, pp. 222-224, italics added)

What does it mean to ask questions? In the case of the Freedom Writers, questions were essential for their re-education, transformation, and moral freedom. From *Freedom Writers Diary* (1995),

"For the first time I heard a teacher take a question seriously."

(Entry #40, p.77).

Maria's questions…

In a PrimeTime Live! segment (1989), Connie Chung asks Maria Reyes, the undisputed firebrand of room 203,

"What is the greatest gift Erin Gruwell gave you?"

Maria responds,

"A second chance. A second chance to make my life better."

34

In the documentary film, *Freedom Writers: Voices from an Undeclared War* (Ankers, 2014), Maria tells how at first she'd refused to read *The Diary of Anne Frank*. How when she'd first saw the cover photograph of Anne, the face of a teenage girl that haunts us because we can read what history has written on it, all Maria saw was another white face that meant nothing to her except the same racial disparity. Just to spite Ms G, Maria started reading, but as she read she recognized how much she had in common with Anne's predicament – Maria was fully cognizant of *"… why the caged bird sings."* Then Maria learns Anne dies in the end, which totally contradicts her gangsta logic. Furious with Ms G, she enters the classroom and like a gauntlet throws down the book.

"Why didn't you tell me Anne Frank didn't make it?!"

Once again Ms G is dumbstruck. She'd assumed everyone knew Anne Frank died in a concentration camp.

Darrius was in the classroom when Maria burst in. Like Maria this Freedom Writer had also been in juvie hall, had minimal expectations for his life expectancy on the mean streets of Long Beach, and as well as little faith in the educational system. With his Ph.D. from the streets, Darrius, calmly and wisely responds to Maria's question,

"Anne did *make it, Maria. She'll live forever because she wrote about it…"*

Maria would find her own voice by writing about her life as Anne had[14]. At the climax of a speech Maria delivered at Marymount University (where I currently work) to a packed auditorium of professors and students she proclaimed, "Reading and writing changed me because it gave me choices!" (Reyes, Marymount University, 11/15/10). Becoming literate gives the oppressed the power of choices, choices that lead to changing themselves and then changing their world (cf., Freire, 1995). It's been said this is why we read. To read high-powered literature such as *Hamlet* or *Portrait of a Lady*, is to ponder who we are, to see ourselves reflected in Hamlet of Isabel Porter and then proceed to change ourselves (Edmundson, 2008). Becoming and being literate is transformational, not stagnation. Literacy leads to action and change. Goethe, philosopher and prodigious reader, said it took him a lifetime to become literate.

Maria had asked Ms G for a copy of *The Diary of Anne Frank* in Spanish because her mother wanted to read about the girl who changed her daughter's life[15]. Certainly it wasn't theory and research-based best practices that rescued Maria and the Freedom Writers from becoming drive-by statistics. Literacy was their life raft. Did the power of curiosity, asking questions, and literacy transformed Ms G's students? In *Pedagogy of the Oppressed* Freire defines praxis as "reflection and action directed at the structure to be transformed...Through praxis oppressed people can acquire a critical awareness of their own condition,

---

[14] Maria's story is central to the plot of the movie version of *Freedom Writers Diary*.

[15] FYI, Maria also made it perfectly clear in her speech at Marymount that she didn't fully credit Ms G for changing her life, from angry Latina to outspoken activist, she proclaimed, "*I chose to change.*"

and, with their allies, struggle for liberation… and to change oppressive structures" (1970, p. 60).

In *Freedom Writers: Voices from an Undeclared War* (Ankers, 2014) Maria asks another heuristic question, "If a good person like Anne doesn't make it then what hope is there for someone like me, a bad person?" But when faced with a moral dilemma as she faced in the courtroom, Maria learned from *Anne Frank's Diary* she had a choice -- to do the gang thing or do the right thing. On the printed page she saw herself, she chose to change, and then she changed her world.

From Freire to eternite….

The awakening of the Freedom Writers' innate curiosity and questions combined with Ms G's uncanny sense of what was at-stake, her impeccable with-it-ness[16], her unstoppable advocacy, her behind-the-scenes machinations and magic, created a swarm of action and reciprocal learning. The stars aligned above Wilson High School, room 203, and the universe conspired to produce a miracle from the clash between a white teacher-in-polka-dots-and-pearls and the bottom-of-the-barrel students who didn't belong, the uneducable, the damaged goods, the rejects, the hopeless, the disengaged. Who knew their irritants would become an infinite string of lustrous pearls? Would combine just the right alchemy to precipitate a curriculum of hope?

As these students come from backgrounds that are very difficult, I think that this gives them the ability to see certain social realities

---

[16] "Withitness" is a term in teacher education that essentially means "having eyes in back of your head," alert to what's totally going on in the classroom.

with more clarity: justice, the marked differences between violence and love. I see their potential to create criticisms and questions with more meaning. *Because they have experienced very difficult things, they are not going to be afraid and they are going to have a very strongest base to be critical of things.*

(Lisbeida, in Cole, 2010, p. xxxi, my italics)

Students with PhDs from the street have their own ways of knowing. They need teachers who will give them a chance or maybe a second chance. A chance to question, a chance to change, a chance to hope. Equal education opportunity for all students may require self-sacrifice, idealism, and creativity....if not outright insurgency. Dewey's vision (1907) for excellent education opportunity for all children requires a pedagogical stance beyond the realm of business-as-usual – let me venture to say, perhaps somewhere in the clouds of unknowing over the rainbow, where despair, fear, and alienation withstand the travails of a yellow brick road that finally leads to hope, courage, and belonging.

It takes a village to raise a child. To educate them takes magic, a revolution, or a miracle. Take your pick.

References

- Aarons, M. P., Natriello, G., & McDill, E.L. (1989). The changing nature of the disadvantaged population: Current dimensions and future trends. *Educational Researcher*, 18 (5). pp. 16-22.

- Anker, D. (Director). (2014). *Freedom Writers: Voices from an undeclared war* [Documentary film]. USA: Freedom Writers Foundation.

- Ball, D. (2015). Postcards to Freedom Writers. unpublished manuscript.

- Ball, D. (1999). *Teaching Jaymes literacy.* Unpublished doctoral dissertation, University of Virginia, Charlottesville, VA.

- Barr, R.D. & Parret, W.H. (2001). *Hope at last for at-risk and violent youth: K-12 programs that work.* Boston: Allyn & Bacon.

- Chung, C. Donaldson, S, Campos, R., Durning, T. (Producers/ Reporters). (1989, April, 15). "Freedom Writers" [news segment]. *In PrimeTime Live.* New York: American Broadcast Company.

- Cole, M. (2010). Revolutionary pedagogy and the twenty-first century socialism in `Bolivian Republic of Venezuela. in *Critical service-learning as revolutionary pedagogy*, Porfilio, B.J. & Hickman, H. Eds. Charlotte, NC: Information Age Pub.

- Darling-Hammond, L. (1997). *The right to learn.* San Francisco: Jossey-Bass.

- Dewey, J. (1907). *School and Society.* Chicago: Univ. of Chicago Press.

- Du Bois, W.E.B. (1949). *The freedom to learn.* Midwest Journal 2 (Winter, 1949) 9-11.

- Edmundson, E. (2004). *Why read?* NYC: Bloomsbury Publishing.

- Edwards, P. A., Pleasants, H. M. & Franklin, S.H. (1999). *A Path to Follow: Learning to listen to parents.* West Port, CT: Heineman.

- Freedom Writers & Gruwell, E. (1998). *Freedom Writers diary.* NYC: Broadway Books.

- Freire, P. (2001). *Pedagogy of freedom. Ethics, democracy, and civic courage.* Lanham, MD: Rowman & Littlefield.

- Freire, P. (2000). *Pedagogy of the oppressed.* Revised 30th anniversary edition. NYC: Continuum.

- Freire, P. (1998a). *Teachers as cultural workers: Letters to those who teach.* Boulder, CO: Westview Press.

- Freire, P. Araújo-Freire, A. M. & Macedo, D. M. (1998b). *The Paulo Freire reader.* NYC: Continuum.

- Freire, P. & Araújo-Freire, A. M. (1994). *Pedagogy of hope: Reliving pedagogy of the oppressed.* NYC: Continuum.

- Freire, P. & Macedo, D. (1987). *Literacy: Reading the word and the world.* South Hadley, MA: Bergen & Garvey Pub.

- Gates, H.L, Jr. (2009). Our roots: *How 10 extraordinary African Americans reclaimed their past.* NYC: Crown Publishers.

- Gruwell, E. & Freedom Writer Teachers. (2009). *Teaching hope, Stories from the Freedom Writer teachers.* NYC: Broadway.

- Gruwell, E. & The Freedom Writers Foundation (2007). *The Freedom Writers Diary Teacher's guide.* NYC: Broadway.

- Hallahan, D. P. & Kauffman, J. M. & Pullen, P.C. (2012). *Exceptional learners: An introduction to special education (12th ed.).* Boston: Allyn and Bacon.

- Holzer, J. (1992). *Green table* [Text inscribed in granite]. Stuart Collection, UC San Diego, San Diego, CA.

- Kerr, M. (2010). The right way to assess teachers' performance. www.washingtonpost.com/wp-dyn/content/ article//2010/ 06/17/AR2010661740565.html

- Kozol, J. (2005). *The shame of the nation*. NYC: Crown.

- LaGravenese, R. (Director). (2007). *Freedom Writers* [Film]. USA: Paramount Pictures.

- Mark, L. (2011). Why we need to stop dissing The Help. retrieved 8/3/2012 http://www.huffingtonpost.com/lois-alter-mark/the-help criticism_b_934792.html?ir%3DEntertainment.

- Murray, C. & Naranjo, J. (2008). Poor, black, learning disabled, and graduating: An investigation of factors and processes associated with school completion among high-risk urban youth. *Remedial & Special Education*, 29: 145-160.

- Murray, C. & Zvoch, K. (2011). Teacher-Student relationships among behaviorally at-risk African-American youth from low-income backgrounds: Student perceptions, teacher perceptions, and socioemotional adjustment correlates. *Journal of Emotional and Behavioral Disorders*, 19(1) 41-54.

- Nolen, M. (2011). Critical education: The need for reform and a place to begin. Unpublished Masters thesis. Arizona State University,

- Pianta, R.C. & Walsh, D.J. (1996). *High-risk children in schools*. New York: Routledge.

- Rose, M. (2005). *Lives on the boundaries: A moving account of the struggles and achievements of America's educationally unprepared*. NYC: Penguin Books.

- Rosen, P. (Producer/Director). (1989). *Understanding learning disabilities: Frustration, Anxiety & tension, the F.A.T. city workshop*, [filmed workshop designed and presented by LaVoie, R.D.] USA: Eagle Hill Outreach.

- Shorris, E. (1998). *The new American blues, a journey through poverty to democracy*. NYC: W.W. Norton & Co.

- Stein, R. (2009). Research links poor kids' stress, brain impairment. *The Washington Post*. 4/6/09. p. A 6.

- Thomas-El, S. (2003). *I choose to stay: A black teacher refuses to desert the inner city*. NYC: Dafina Books.

About the author

Doug Ball: Since 1984 I have taught in a variety of settings including correctional facilities, community-based adult literacy programs, public schools, and for the past 15 years a professor in university teacher education programs. As a Freedom Writer Teacher I have been involved in several projects including writing an entry for *Teaching Hope, Stories from the Freedom Writer Teachers* and working with the team to edit the book as well. I also contributed to the teacher's manual and student workbook for Scholastic's *Off the Record* reading series. As a professor my research has taken me to Nicaragua where I have studied the *Cruzada Nacional de Alfabetización*, the historic adult literacy campaign instigated in 1980 after the Sandinista Revolution with the help of Paulo Freire.

Barb Fouts-Melnychuk

It has just begun!

Can you remember a teacher who changed your view of the world? What if I told you that by using The Freedom Writers' methods and resources I was able to transform great to extraordinary, motivate both "at risk" and gifted learners, as well have students beg to learn more. The Freedom Writers' approach provided me with the tools to engage students at a level that allowed me the opportunity to explicitly teach reading and writing strategies. The outcome ultimately resulted in students taking more ownership for their learning as they recognized that they were connected and capable.

For me the transformation in my students started with a small request: an appeal for just a bit of my time at lunch. Looking into the faces of these teenagers who used to claim that they didn't care about school, stirred emotions deep down within me. Naturally I found myself rushing through lunch to listen to these, once reluctant, students and their latest idea. They began by describing a documentary they watched on the weekend that paralleled the novel being read in class. The only problem they pointed out, was how many letters would they need to write and how would they get the finances to bring the people from the documentary to Dickensfield School for all the students?

"I don't know," I replied, smiling as I ventured onto the web searching for a contact name to start the writing campaign.

* * *

…This student enthusiasm all started with my grade 8 Language Arts class, in the fall of 2008. This class consisted of 19 students, all who had learning difficulties: many with negative behavior issues that portrayed the image of "the kids who just don't care about school." My assessment of the students indicated that 85% of them had reading and writing levels between a 3-4-grade level. I was looking for something to help me deal with that "we-hear-you-but-we-don't-care-or-understand-glazed-look" from their faces. I had recently watched the movie The Freedom Writers, about Erin Gruwell, a teacher that changed the lives and academic achievement of 150 students from Long Beach California. I decided this movie was going to be the inspirational tool that would hook my students and make them love learning. Not only did it hook them, they were so inspired by the stories from The Freedom Writers that they took to starting a letter writing campaign. Approximately 165 letters in total were written, all in an attempt to bring Erin Gruwell and The Freedom Writers to Edmonton. I had never witnessed my students that excited or that willing to work on any project. Also the excitement paid big dividend in my students' academic achievement. By the end of April 2009, 17 of the 19 students were within a year or were at grade level for both reading and writing: all because they got excited and saw purpose to what they were learning.

The biggest surprise though came from my gifted French Immersion students. After four months of persistent inquiries and a diagnosis of pneumonia, I finally agreed to forfeit curricular time to watch The Freedom Writers. Ironically these students also took their writing to new levels, as they insisted that they had to become part of our letter writing campaign. The icing on our cake was a phone call that came at the end of a day in May 2009. The call was from California. I was with my grade 8 French Immersion Language Arts class when "California" showed up on my call display. I started jumping up and down yelling, "It's California, its California," as my students, prompted me to pick up the phone. I very calmly answered, pretending I was not at all fazed as I was told that Erin Gruwell had accepted Edmonton Public Schools' invitation and when was a good time for the Freedom Writers to come to Alberta? I don't actually remember what I said, except I politely hung up and my class-room became as loud as the Super Bowl stadium at the end of a Championship game.

The students kept jumping up and down screaming, "WE DID IT! WE DID IT," and they had. A group of grade 8 students labeled "low achievers", and four groups of "academically enriched" kids brought one of the most extraordinary teachers and humanitarians I have ever had the pleasure of meeting to Edmonton, in January 2010. That is when Erin's philosophy of Engagement, Enlightenment and Empowerment made me real-ize that The Freedom Writers' methods took what I was doing well and made my strategies and techniques out of this world; all because one grade 8 boy who asked "Why can't we bring the Freedom Writers' to Edmonton?" …And the only answer I had, after 20 years of imparting my wisdom was, "I don't know?" I am so glad my students knew what needed to be done, and that they were willing to take on the role of teacher, and show me how to use a web page. Thank goodness they were willing to lead me, as the journey has been life altering, magical and inspir-ing, and it has just began!

About the author

Barb Fouts-Melnychuk has taught junior high, grades 7-9, for 24 years in Edmonton, Alberta, Canada. She started teaching teens that were so traumatized and violent they could not function in a school setting. She specializes in working with behavior disordered students but has branched out and also taught students with learning disabilities, autistic students, the gifted students, students from affluence, all girl and all boy programs and now teaches in a middle class setting made up of mainstream teens with a large percentage of English Language Learners. She found the Freedom Writers while working with a class of grade 8s who were performing at gr. 3 level. The Freedom Writers hooked them and after 2 years all 19 students left grade 9 reading and writing at grade level. Ms. FM, as the students call her, has become more deliberate with her class practices, using the Freedom Writer philosophy to engage and empower all students. She has been astounded at the passion the advanced placement teens, the middle class kids or her students at risk respond with. As the teenagers start to see their writing making a difference their enthusiasm becomes contagious and they transform before her eyes.

Michelle L. Holliday

The Manufactured Factory Model vs. the Empowered Global Humanitarian

> *Unless someone like you cares a whole awful lot, Nothing is going to get better. It's not.*
>
> — Dr. Seuss (*The Lorax*)

With the myriad of responsibilities and mandates placed on public educators today, simply bowing down and teaching to the test can become quite enticing. Standards-based regiments, incessant data analysis, school-wide grade benchmark assessments, and *No Child Left Behind* stipulations all intertwine into a domineering persona in classrooms nationwide. These regulations mentally weigh down the typical teacher and slowly strip away creativity, social justice analysis, student-led inquiry, and project-based learning – all curriculum components that build a collective community within a classroom. Add into this mix the pressure of teaching in an urban setting – where a majority of the students are often impoverished, functioning below grade level performance targets, and sometimes apathetic or hostile to academic and personal growth – and the daily demands of the high school teacher seem rather daunting and hopeless.

The combination of the unique demands of the urban teaching environment, combined with top-heavy directives from the state and national level, manufactures a regimented, superficial, and surface level factory model environment where students are mass produced to pass the test, earn an obligatory grade, acquire the desired diploma, and eventually enter into the "real world" lacking functional 21st Century skills. Similar to any other profession, teaching has numerous obstacles and challenges that can convolute, overwhelm, and slowly disappoint its diligent educators; thus, sometimes reducing once passionate professionals into teachers who resignedly conform to state or administrative directives for the sake of a coveted evaluative score to increase data targets. Even more unfortunate is the teacher, who due to burnout or frustration, instructs without passion or expels minimal effort and creativity regarding lesson plans and relationship building with students. In contrast to other professions, the end "products" that are shipped down the production line in education are fragile young people with impressionable minds. What happens if teachers fail to implement tools for success beyond simple skill building? What if teachers are so focused on getting students to pass THAT test or meet THAT standard within the designated content area, and in the process forget to inspire and empower students to get to know one another and the world outside of the confines of a multiple choice test or state mandated standardized exam? What are the resounding consequences when teachers fail to fuel students with appealing experiences, interactive dialogue, and reflective learning that produce well-rounded and socially conscious young adults – those who are ready and willing to become active, productive, and contributing members to their society? Teenagers who are about to survive the next phase of this intimidating world need to be armed and equipped with effective tools, knowledge, and reflective humanitarian skills which allow them to function both successfully *and* compassionately with one another. The Freedom Writers methodology trains and rejuvenates teachers to reach beyond state mandated testing practices to instead apply a thought-provoking and inclusive curriculum which plant seeds for positive, self-reflective change coupled with social justice inquiry analysis and action.

Erin Gruwell's innovative teacher training program, The Freedom Writer's Institute, is a stark contrast to the factory model approach that plague countless schools. Currently, 400 international teachers have been meticulously trained to trigger a ripple effect of positive change in their classrooms through novel teaching methods, kinesthetic activities, and reflective student interactions. Erin's unorthodox methods challenge students to get out of their seats, push aside personal and societal prejudices, and communicate both verbally and through the written word, in hopes of producing genuine understanding and appreciation for the interconnectedness that can exist within the individual classroom and its inhabitants. Developing a familial community of positive and compassionate learners helps students function strongly and interdependently amid a chaotic and misguided external society. Purposefully embedding a hidden agenda of moral practices and humanistic experiences into the classroom learning environment plants vital seeds of change that will later germinate into stimulated, reflective, and sustained student growth.

Instead of forcing a teacher-dominated hierarchy where students "sit and get" content in an one dimensional, direct instruction approach, Erin's lesson plans ask students to therapeutically reflect on their lives through journal writing, which improves overall writing skills while also emotionally connecting fellow classmates. Sharing personal stories, successes, tragedies, and dreams in the written form allows students to feel included, heard, and universally understood. Journal entries are completed while students simultaneously read *The Freedom Writers Diary,* where they analyze, discuss, and reflect on their personal stories juxtaposed with those of the Freedom Writer authors. Kinesthetic and visual activities like the Coat of Arms project work conjunctively with journal writing as a nonthreatening, introspective icebreaker. Participation in this project invites students to portray themselves both on paper and by oral presentation; students are then invited to publically display their final products for all to enjoy. The Line Game, a culminating activity of the institute's curriculum, challenges students to take a stand and share their life experiences without saying a single word. It is by far the most impactful tactic taught by Erin and duplicated in classrooms worldwide. This sole activity breaks down the final barriers that separate and isolate students, consequently freeing them to transform into a team of unified learners working jointly toward academic and personal achievement. Once such limiting barriers have been destroyed, the curriculum then challenges students to reach beyond their classroom and become activists for positive change.

Becoming activists for positive change forces teachers to extinguish the archaic factory model approach and start generating a classroom which promotes common humanity and global activism. Social justice inquiry and analysis forces teens to look outside of their limited, microcosmic lives to instead experience the broader, diverse world. Studying current events, controversial topics, and unjust events from the past and present are all tactics that can be easily tied to standards-based learning; however, instead of just focusing on acing the unit test and then moving on, students are instead summoned to think critically, synthesize, question, and discover information which often extends beyond grade level expectations and parameters.

Student-led inquiry, project-based learning, and daily analysis of historical and current events allow students to become fully immersed into their global society, producing another thread of inclusion at the most important level. Guest speakers, Skype sessions, movie and documentary analysis, nonfiction article reviews, student debates, and community action projects should all be combined into an interactive, thriving classroom that is fully safe and transparent for all learners. How can one study a topic such as the Holocaust without recognizing that such atrocities happened beyond World War II and are still occurring today? Inviting an iconic guest speaker like *Hotel Rwanda's* protagonist, Paul Rusesabagina, or Skyping with a Freedom Writer teacher like Issa Vianney Sikubwabo, a Rwandan genocide survivor who currently teaches orphans in his native country, can help students grasp the gritty devastation of genocide from the lips of the survivors themselves. How can one study prejudice and equal rights without talking about homophobia and introducing stories that touch hearts and change perspectives regarding the LGBT community? Matthew Boger and Tim Zaal's Oscar nominated documentary, *Facing Fear*, illustrates a man who changed his ways after a brutal attack on a gay youth; ironically, both men now work together and speak publicly about the incident. They have also written an autobiographical account of their inspirational story, and students need to have access to such pieces. However, sometimes a guest speaker cannot speak directly to a classroom of students due to age, health, or death. Such is the case with the acclaimed documentary *Matthew Shepard is a Friend of Mine*, which eloquently weaves a portrait of a slain man's life and murder due to the insidious prejudice of homophobia. Michele Josue, a former classmate of Matthew's and Director of the film, brought Mathew's voice back, and teachers need to embrace the story and share its powerful visual message.

Guest speakers, current event analysis, and social justice themed literature and nonfiction pieces all work collaboratively with grade level curricula to spark student concern and action through project-based learning opportunities. In Freedom Writer teacher-led classrooms nationwide, countless students participate in inventive projects that involve both local and global connections and lessons. Whether it is creating a Pen Pal program between a stateside school and one in Africa, organizing a field trip to the Simon Wiesenthal Museum of Tolerance, collecting millions of Band-Aids to symbolically represent the lives lost in the Holocaust, or participating in community service projects to beautify and rejuvenate the community, students are activity engaged, invested, and inspired to break the mold of teenage narcissism and apathy to instead become invested global humanitarians. Surrounded by the cutthroat, indifferent, and greedy culture that exists today, empathy is a skill that must be taught to students. Such projects instill this vital component that is absent from content mastery, but is important to intrapersonal and external growth. In addition to fostering empathy and hope, such projects seamlessly mold students into pragmatic activists who are productive and contributing members to their macro society.

Creating positive reflection, change, and purposeful student activism through introspective writing, social injustices analysis, and service learning projects can seem like a daunting task for the everyday classroom teacher. Ultimately, promoting and helping to create a righteous society is arduous because student inquiry sometimes doesn't expand or even occur outside of the four walls of an English or history classroom. However, the Freedom Writer Teacher's job is to push students outside of their comfort zones to see, question, and think critically of the world and its diverse inhabitants; all of its glory, shame, and unanswered questions are part of this inquiry process of growth that plants the seeds for hope and enlightenment within students, enabling a personal metamorphosis to take root.

About the author

Michelle Holliday is a native of Lancaster, PA and moved to Richmond, Indiana in 1994, where she attended Richmond High School and graduated in 1997. At Ball State University, she majored in English Secondary Education with a dual minor in Communications and Theater. Michelle obtained her Master's in Education degree from Indiana Wesleyan University in 2004. In 2011, Michelle was selected to become a Freedom Writer Teacher, a program that has bettered her teaching and life. Currently, Michelle is wrapping up her 13th year of teaching English at the secondary level; she feels blessed to work with innovative and supportive colleagues in the Freshman Academy Program at Richmond High School. In her spare time, Michelle enjoys reading, watching movies, dancing in Zumba class, eating out, socializing with friends and family, traveling to warm places, and spending time with her two adorable sons (Benjamin and Drew) and her husband, Ryan. One quote that epitomizes Michelle's teaching philosophy is, "The mediocre teacher tells. The good teacher explains. The superior teacher demonstrates. The great teacher inspires" (William Arthur Ward). Michelle's primary objective as an educator is to motivate her students to become compassionate, knowledgeable, and reflective citizens; the Freedom Writer Methodology has been an instrumental resource in accomplishing this endearing goal.

Brett Mitchell
Relationship

Crying in my office, she just disclosed that she had been sexually abused by a family member. I knew I now had to call Youth Protection services and start the all too familiar process yet again. Just an hour before, I had another young student tell me that he was hungry and he did not have a lunch with him because his parents are not around in the mornings to make it for him and he had forgotten to do it himself. I knew tonight would be another restless night for me. But let me back up first.

A few years ago, on one of those very rare evenings when my wife and I had both actually had our classes prepared for the next day, our own children were in bed sleeping soundly, our correcting was complete and paperwork up to date (yes, very rare indeed), we were watching television when my wife came upon the movie *Freedom Writers*. I was surprised when she told me she had never seen it, so we decided to watch part of it. After getting caught up in the film's plot, rather than taking the opportunity for an early night like smart people would, we stayed up much later than we should have and finished the film.

We are far removed from the gang violence of 1980's East LA, being the principal of a small rural school in Quebec, Canada and my wife an English Second Language teacher in our local small college, but we both recognized the methods used by Ms Erin Gruwell could be easily adapted to our reality. I had already used some activities in my previous teaching life in Sydney, Australia, so I soon found myself with a renewed enthusiasm for the Freedom Writer methodology.

Together, my wife and I set about creative ways to engage her students around the Freedom Writer methodology, developing her upcoming semester course around the film. Using this film and *Pay It Forward*, we developed various classes and projects that had the students looking beyond their own culture by taking a closer look at the social issues our region faced, and her evaluations had the students actually doing good for the community. By the end of the course, many of her students told her that it was the most motivating course they had ever sat. Even 18 months later, I was at the local swimming pool with my daughter when one of the life guards recognized us and could not stop talking about my wife's course and how much she loved it, especially the surprise Skype interview with Ms Tiffony Jacobs, one of the original Freedom Writers, at the end of the course. To this day, my wife swears it was her best semester ever.

After helping my wife implement the Freedom Writer methodology into her college courses, I turned to my school, which had already grown dramatically since my appointment as principal. When I took over the administration of the school, I knew nothing about being a principal, with the position thrust onto me when the previous principal resigned. The school was in trouble and the only thing I knew how to do well was teach, that meant keeping the kids engaged and to develop a sense of trust. I set about creating a turn around. We rebuilt the school's programs, revisited its policies, wrote grants and developed partnerships, all with the aim of engaging the students. We went from a 25% graduation rate to 100%, doubling the enrolment, and watched as literacy and math success rates increased, while absenteeism and discipline problems dropped. This turn-around gained some attention, and so it was with humility I accepted the request to present our success at a provincial principal's conference.

So, there I was, ready to enter the conference's opening ceremony when I finally had the time to read the program, only to discover that Ms Gruwell was our keynote speaker, at which I promptly texted this to my wife, making her very jealous. This was not my original intention, but an added bonus. When the event organizer saw me and offered to introduce me to Ms Gruwell, I was elated and I took the opportunity to talk with her briefly, expressing my admiration for her work and explaining its recent impact on my wife and I and our students. After her emotional presentation and lining up for a signed copy of her book, I discovered that the association organizing the conference was going to sponsor one person to fly to Los Angeles and work with Ms Gruwell, becoming the ambassador of her program of the English school system of Quebec. I was fortunate enough to be the one chosen.

A few short months later, I was flying back home after an intense week of workshops that had me on an emotional rollercoaster. I had the opportunity to work with and witness Ms Gruwell utilize her activities in a classroom setting, meet with many of the original Freedom Writers, visit places that were in the film, and meet Holocaust survivors and gay rights activists. But most incredibly it was my peers, the 23 other participants who were taking the course with me that I became most inspired by. People that had survived the Rwandan Genocide or were working tirelessly for the Anne Frank House, others working in Germany, Denmark, Canada, and all across the United States, each of them with incredible stories of their own. I still look back at the photos of that trip with great fondness, my favorite being a picture of my German colleague, Mr. Jörg Knüfken, sitting down and chatting with a Holocaust survivor, Ms Renee Firestone. During lunch, Jörg was sitting opposite me, being unusually quiet when I asked him if he was ok. He told me about his discomfort, being German and having the focus of the morning's session being Nazi Germany, that as much as he wanted to talk with Ms Firestone, he was scared to offend her. At this, Ms Gruwell grabbed his arm and dragged him over, sat him down next to her, introduced them and they began a lengthy conversation. At this moment, I had more faith in humanity and its ability for reconciliation than ever before. If this man, who was uncomfortable for what his countrymen once did, and this woman, who experienced such horrors at the hands of the Nazi regime were able to speak comfortably, even after she has freshly retold her story to us, then there is hope.

I came back to work that September armed full of ideas for my school, training for my staff, new materials for everyone to read or try and contacts I knew would be inspirational for our students. And so began our school's true Freedom Writer journey. The fantastic staff at our school quickly jumped on board, with many utilizing activities from the *Teacher's Guide* and the general philosophy, quick favorites being the *Line Game, Frootloop Bingo* and *Sandwich*. Throughout the school year we focused on a Genocide theme for our Elementary Grade 5 to Secondary 5, covering the Holocaust, Rwanda and Bosnia, amongst others. We read books, did activities, researched, developed projects and created a Facebook group between our students and those from a Rwandan school for orphans. We Skyped with Freedom Writers, Holocaust and various genocide survivors, even Ms

Gruwell herself, and over summer, we hosted the Anne Frank House travelling exhibition with a number of our students and parents being volunteer guides.

Other activities promoted in the Freedom Writer methodology such as journal writing, helped our students with their language development. The majority of our students (90%+) are Second Language learners and we are therefore always looking for ways to help our students enjoy reading and writing. We soon found the students instantly engaged in anything we labeled as a Freedom Writer activity. Each of these activities were easy enough to follow, and could be incorporated into almost any class, I was even using *Frootloop bingo* in my Math classes to help reinforce vocabulary. But, what we discovered from using the methodology was much deeper than just classroom activities that everyone enjoyed, it was the relationship that we developed with the students that was our biggest surprise.

The Line Game opened up some of our teachers' eyes to what our students were facing day to day. Poverty and homelessness, violence in the home and sexual abuse, suicide and cutting were all things that most thought were rare in our beautiful, quiet region, let alone in our own school. Our snacks and breakfast program took on a whole new meaning. Our incredible sports program, where we take the students out of the school for skiing, golf, tennis, karate, weight training, Zumba, and the like, provided the life-long healthy lifestyle skills the students so desperately needed. The extra-curricular activities like camping, canoeing and trips to New York gave the students the chance to experience things that many would otherwise not be able to afford. Taking the students out of the classroom also allowed the students to connect with each other and their teachers on a whole new level, seeing each other in a new light, helping them develop a newfound level of respect for each other. It opened up the students to each other's lives, many of them previously believing they were alone in their struggles. They discovered that everyone has their own issues and that they are not alone, with many having gone on to develop a strong sense of empathy for others.

Our school, with its tiny population, only 23 when I started there, now at 81, always had a family feel about it. We are the only English school in over a 2-hour travel radius, surrounded by French speaking Quebec, with less than 1% of the population who speak English. Our village hosts about 100 English speakers year round, yet most of our students come from the surrounding region, with almost all students having at well over an hour bus ride to and from school each day. We have very little access to English services, be it Health Care, Psychologists, or even our own educational consultants and directors. With these hurdles and the extreme isolation, we have developed a culture of family in our school and community. I know what my students are doing on the weekend, their pet's names, their favorite hockey team, etc. and they know everything about me. This has advantages, as we get to know our students very well, allowing us to really design our curriculum around their needs. On the other hand, getting a phone call from a parent on a Saturday evening while trying taking what little family time I do have has its drawbacks.

Similar to Ms G.'s reality, this deep involvement and commitment to my work has taken a toll on my personal life. Throughout my regular day at the school, between teaching (yes, I still teach a 50% load while being the principal), and the time I take to be with the students, I never have time for my paperwork and emails, this is done in the evenings, once my children are asleep. My lesson preparations are done on Sundays. I have almost no social life, and my children have continually complained that I am too busy to play with them, with my face continually buried in my laptop. My wife has complained about those late night or weekend work related phone calls and that we never have time for us. My parents complain that they do not hear enough from me and my own health has suffered, weight wise and I now wear glasses from all the hours I spend in front of the computer, not just with the principal duties, but researching and teaching myself the best way to teach or counsel these students. The late nights I spend completing my work and when I finally do get to bed, the restless nights spent thinking about my students and what they face day-to-day, trying to find the best way to help them. But, on those odd days, when you do get a thank you, a Facebook message from a former student telling you how successful they have become, or watching that particular student receive their high school diploma and entry into college when so many others had given up on him, you know it is all worth it.

We have found that the teachers who have embraced the Freedom Writer methodology have developed relationships that have gone beyond the obvious. Students have developed a deeper sense of trust in their teachers. Students have been more open and willing to disclose and discuss the issues they may be facing with their teachers and peers. I have had students come to me with the most unexpected questions, ones that students have never brought to me before, let alone to a principal, from depression and drugs, to parental problems and sex education. I have had students disclose information about poverty, self-abuse and sexual abuse. I have had students recognizing that they are in a frame of mind that is not conductive to learning and rather than walking into the classroom and getting into trouble, they will come to me and my office for some down time.

Recently, I had a student who was having a bad day, come to my office just to escape the hustle and bustle of her regular day for a few minutes. She had been through a particularly tough year, both at home and in school, and we had discussed many of her issues over the course of the year. I believed I had a source of advice and comfort for her. This particular day, as we chatted about her frustration over another student in her class that she was ready to punch, she casually informed me that had I not been there for her, she would have been dead by now. While she is still struggling with many aspects in her life, she is set to graduate this year and has some goals for post-secondary life.

Despite having students crying in my office disclosing horror stories of abuse, despite the sleepless nights and the extra workload I put onto myself, I still believe firmly in the Freedom Writer methodology of connecting with the students, connecting them to the world around them and making the curriculum relevant to their lives. By taking this much more holistic approach to a student's learning than the traditional pure sharing of academic knowledge, this methodology has been a leading role in the success of our small school, of my own classes and of our students. Thank you Ms Gruwell, the original Freedom Writers and my fellow Freedom Writer Teachers

About the author:

Brett Mitchell: Born in Sydney, Australia, I became a Mathematics and Computer teacher and taught for eight years in Sydney. I met my now wife, Chantal, in 1998 and we spent two years together in Australia before we both moved to her home town of Matane, Quebec, Canada. I taught for five years in the small rural English school, Metis Beach, before becoming the school's principal with a 50% teaching load in 2006, which I still hold today. My wife and I have three gorgeous children and I became a Freedom Writer Teacher in June 2013.

Christine Maraist Neuner, E. Ed.

Cautionary Tales: The Folk Tales and Fairy Tales Our Mothers Told Us
A Cautionary Tale Unit

It is noteworthy to include folk tales and fairy tales in the curriculum for students of all ages. Much can be learned from the tales. It has been noted that most of the students were not read fairy tales as children and much was lost as mothers as rule-givers. In my childhood my mother read Grimm's fairytales and made up stories of her own—all of which had a moral for the day. She told stories of heroics that were duly rewarded, stories of caution and safety.

To begin this unit, I ask the students to write about their favorite fairy tale. I remind them that Disney has made animated films based on the fairy tales. In their journals they can recollect their favorite Disney-version of a tale. However, in Louisiana some of my students have written interesting folktales from the Louisiana Bayous for this part of the unit. They tell of the *cauchemar* and the *loup garou*. The *cauchemar* is the little man who will sit on one's chest as they sleep at night and suck out the person's breath or a nightmare. The *loup garou* is a French legend of a human who changes into a wolf at his or her own will. After this exercise, we start to look into the types of tales. At the end of the unit, the students use the materials to create their own cautionary tale as a final activity.

There are various types of tales from around the world our children should know. There are household tales that come from home, from people who tell fantastic stories about how life was in days gone by. One such story is a lullaby my great grandmother sang to me just as she sang it to her granddaughter and daughter. Another such story is about a poor mother known as La Illarona who becomes the antithesis of a good mother. They are both cautionary tales to warn children to stay close to home or the wilderness would surely swallow them up.

Another form of cautionary tale is the fairy tale. Traditionally a village story-teller would spin these tales in order to scare the children into obedience. There are the Grimm's fairy tales that echo the Perrault tales which more than likely echo from older myths. According to the Aborigines of Australia, their earliest ancestors created the folk tale. The tradition has it that these early ancestors covered themselves with clay and wandered about Australia. As they went they called out the names of everything they encountered: animals, plants, hills, rocks, streams. In this way the ancestors sang the world into being. These pathways are known as "song-lines." The song is like a map, if you know the song. (*Elements of Literature*, p. 865)

Folktales are the body of people's popular, traditional knowledge that also includes their proverbs, nursery rhymes, folk songs, riddles superstitions, and cautionary tales. There are recurring motifs and symbols in the tales that make them universal. There are stories about the nature of wisdom, stories that explain how and why the world came to be the way it is. There are tales of wonder and magic, tales of trickery and deceit, and tales of caution. There are, for example, over four hundred versions of Cinderella worldwide. Although not all folktales and fairy tales have all these motifs, most do have a good dose of them.

The symbols are so numerous to provide here, but Juan Cirlot's *A Dictionary of Symbols* is available to derive meanings of the various symbols for the myriad tales we have in our fairy tales, folktales, and cautionary tales. For the three stories I have chosen as examples of the cautionary tales, the important symbols are listed in the appendix. The motifs are also important to follow in these tales. The chart also lists the motifs found in such stories with a checklist of what is found in the three stories presented.

The reason the telling of the tales is important is that it can save a child from harm as the cautionary tales depict. But, as the masters of Taoism say, society could be held together if individuals adhere to tradition and morality. Taoism stresses family, duty, obedience, respect for elders, and proper conduct in social relations. As the Tao master dictates:

> *Where there is nobility in spirit, there is beauty of character.*
> *Where there is beauty in character, there is harmony in the home.*
> *Where there is a harmonious home, there is an orderly nation.*
> *Where there is an orderly nation, there is peace in the world.*
> --from *The Great Learning*

Cautionary tales give the warning of course, but they also make distinctions between proper and improper social conduct. The stories give the reader what the social values and mores are to be followed. They demonstrate the rewards of humility and simplicity. There is a relationship man must see between himself and nature as well. This is taught through the yin-yang balance of the world. Yang is the masculine side—the sunny side. Yin is the feminine side—the dark side. Each half is cut in the middle of the opposing half to symbolize that every mode must contain within it the germ of its antithesis. It is a constantly spinning wheel of the universe which shows us the continuous metamorphoses of the world. (Cirlot, p. 380)

To exemplify these ideals, three tales come to mind which shows the importance of perpetuating the tales of our mothers into the next millennium. Follow along as the tales are spun and look for the symbols and the motifs. To start my lesson on fairy tales and folktales, I ask the students to relate any tales that they may have heard or read themselves. Most of them retell the Disney animations of fairy tales they have seen as children. These cleaned-up versions of the fairy tale start the conversation, and they look at the charts for motifs and symbols (see appendix) to discuss their meanings. Then, using the motif and symbol charts, the students are asked to write their own fairy tale or folktale. They must remember to have all the components we have discussed in class using the tales they recall. Now to the three tales the students have read:

The Illarona[17]

If you have watched ABC's *Grimm*, a version of the tale of the Illarona was told as part of the mystery the Portland police had to solve. The story is from Mexico which was usually told to the children of migrant workers. The story came to me from my sister-in-law whose parents had told her tale when she and her siblings were younger.

---

[17] As told by Tomas Gonsales Neuner

There once was a most beautiful lady in the land. She was very sweet and everyone loved her. However, once the handsome Don Carlos began courting her, she became very vain. At first, the villagers did not fault her. Because she was so beautiful and kind, they thought she deserved such a prize of Don Carlos for a husband. They decided that the sin of pride would pass. Once she married, Don Carlos built for her a most wonderful hacienda in the whole village. It was stucco with whitewashed walls and beautiful green tiles for the roof. It had many rooms filled with handsome furniture from Old Madrid. La Doña Carlos had many parties there where she invited the whole village. When she began to travel, however, she began to change. After meeting so many important people such as Governor Pio Pico of Nuevo España, La Doña Carlos began snubbing her village friends. Yet, the villagers were forgiving as they said she had such a lovely hacienda, of course only the finest people would guest there.

Finally it came to pass that Don and La Doña Carlos were to have a baby. Oh, how the villagers were taken by the happy news. They prepared a great fiesta for the child's birth. They danced and sang about the happy event to arrive in their village. And, when the baby boy was born, what a lovely child he was. He was fat and rolly, healthy with pink cheeks and such big brown eyes with silky lashes ever seen. At first La Doña Carlos was very public with her beautiful child. She would take him out every day with his abuela to show him off to the entire village. She would say, "My baby boy is handsomest of all the children in the village. Why his handsomest of all Nueva España." The villagers would only agree with La Doña Carlos about her child. He WAS the handsome child of all Nueva España. How could he not be? He came from the most handsome parents bother her in Nueva España as well as the old country as far as they were concerned. So, they forgave La Doña Carlos once again for her vanity and pride.

Finally, another great announcement was made from the great hacienda of Don Carlos. They were to have another child. Great ceremonies began once again in the village. The people planned a great fiesta for the child and Don and La Doña Carlos and their new child. She was born as beautiful as her brother was handsome and the whole village rejoiced. La Doña Carlos was so proud of her two beautiful children, she begged Don Carlos to let her take a voyage to Old Spain so she could show them off to her family back in the old world. At first Don Carlos says, "No, my dear, the journey is tool perilous. I would die if anything would happen to you and our dear children. Stay here in Nueva España with me your adoring husband and our adoring villagers. No harm could come to our children with such love as we and they have for them."

La Doña Carlos was not satisfied with his answer/. She was so proud of her beautiful children she wanted to show them off to her family in Spain. She also wanted to brag to her still childless older sister how lucky she was to have her two beautiful children. And, she was so vain, she wanted to show off her still lovely figure to all the admirers she left back home. She went to one of the abuelas who mixed magic to make a spell for her to win Don Carlos' permission to take the trip home.

The abuela told her she would make a potion for her to make Don Carlos bend to her every whim. The old woman agreed to help, but La Doña Carlos must never be prideful again, as she had been doing since her marriage to Don Carlos.

If she did not heed the warning, something horrible would befall her. She would become a sad woman for the rest of her days and the rest of her days would outlive all who know and love her. La Doña Carlos promised she would check her pride and vanity, anything to gain the magic potion to sway Don Carlos to her whim.

The abuela made the potion for her. That evening at dinner, she secretly poured the potion into Don Carlos' wine while they ate. She took great care that the meal would sumptuous so that Don Carlos would be in good cheer. In that way he would enjoy his wine and thus the potion would be drunk. She watched with eager anticipation as he ate his meal and enjoyed his wine. Then, as they walked in their garden, she asked Don Carlos if he reconsider the trip she so wanted to take back to Spain. Without hesitation, Don Carlos said she could go and he would tell the captain of one his many merchant ships to set sail within the month. In that way, La Doña Carlos and her children would see their homeland.

La Doña Carlos was ecstatic with making her plans. She had all the finest clothes made for the children and her. She had the nicest gifts to share with her family in Spain. She would sing the praises of Don Carlos as she showed off the great bounty of the New World thus keeping her word to the abuela. However, just as the ship set sail from the Yucatan, the captain complimented La Doña Carlo and her family. She just started to proudly brag about her beautiful babies when a horrible storm came out of the East. A water spout came and took the ship up into the darkened sky. Then it dropped it and crashed it asunder killing all aboard including the lovely babies of Don Carlos.

However, a sailor from another ship who saw the stormy wreak swore to the day of his death that he saw a woman whisked away on another water spout and dumped in the scrub land of Tulum. He heard such a wail from that he crossed himself a dozen times. There is a saying that she is still with us, but today we call her La Illarona, The Crier, because once she started wailing over her lost babies, she never stopped. If you children ever go too near any wooded area or waterway and hear her doleful cry, run quickly home. That is La Illarona who will think you are her long lost children, and she will consume you with her grief and you will never be seen again. Do not wander too far from home, children, for La Illarona is always near no matter where you are.

The Song: Poor Babes in the Woods[18]

Another cautionary tale comes in the form of folksong. It is an early American story told to children of pioneer families traveling West in the wagon trains. This was a warning to children to stay close to the wagon train at night. If they wandered too far, they could be lost and never found again. It is a woeful tale indeed.

Oh don't you remember a long time ago:
those two little babes, their names I don't know?
Were stolen away on a fine summer's day
And left in the woods, I heard people say.

---

[18] Source *Tales Our Settlers Told,* as sung by Carrie Terhune Reed

Now when it was night,
So sad was their plight.
The moon went down,
The stars gave no light.

They sobbed and the sighed,
And they bitterly cried.
Poor babes in the woods,
They laid down and died.

Now when they were dead,
The robin so red,
Brought strawberry leaves
And over them spread.

Then she sang them a song
The whole day long.
Poor babes in the woods.
Poor babes in the woods.

A sad song indeed, but it probably saved many a children from wandering too far from the wagon train.

Korean Cinderella[19]

The Koreans have one of many Cinderella stories in their culture which shows a parallel of the cultures. It shows the mother

---

[19] Based on Shirley Climo's story

figure as seen in our more Western cautionary tales in the same light.

Little Pear Blossom and her father were very happy together, even though her mother had passed away when she was very little. However, her father felt that his Little Pear Blossom needed a mother and siblings. He was too old to father more children, he thought, so he found a widow with daughters in a neighboring village. He met with the marriage broker, and the two were wed within the year. He dressed her in a beautiful golden hanbok (a Korean dress) and lovely white shoes on her pretty feet. She was a lovely child who was adored by all.

All went well for Pear Blossom her father, her new mother and step-sisters for a while. However, the old man became ill and soon died. Things began to change for Little Pear Blossom. First, she was reduced to a tattered hanbok, a Korean dress, and no shoes. Then she was sent to live with the animals. She made friends with all the animals: the frog, the crickets, the birds and the ox were friendly and kept her company. Finally, she was mad to do all the work as the money was squandered by her step-mother and step-sisters and the servants were let go.

However, Little Pear Blossom made friends with the animals in the shed, and she never complained about the hard work she was to endure. She would wash the clothes, make the meals, scrub the floors, and repair her step-sisters clothing. She did all this with a smile on her face, and she never complained.

One day the family learned of a great feast set out for the local prince. All the unmarried ladies of the village were invited to attend. Little Pear Blossom wanted to go, too. However, her step-mother said, "You can go if you fill this jar with water!" Well, that jar the step-mother handed her was full of holes. How could it ever hold water? Little Pear Blossom sighed, and said to her friend the frog, "Friend Frog, how will I ever get this jar to hold water?" Friend Frog croaked, "No need to fear, Pear Blossom, I will jump in the jar, plug the whole, and the water will stay." With that, he jumped in the jar. "Thank you, Friend Frog; you are truly a great friend, "said Little Pear Blossom. The plug held and the water jar was full to brimming when Little Pear Blossom set the jar down in front of her step-mother.

"Well, that is all well and good, but we need for you to get us rice before we go!" She sent Little Pear Blossom to rice field, but it was full of water. How could she winnow the rice from its stalks if the water was so high? "Oh, Brother Ox, whatever will I do?" she asked. "I cannot get to the rice with so much water surrounding the stalks!" Brother Ox told her not to worry. And with a great snort, he blew the water away from the stalks. Little Pear Blossom thanked Brother Ox for his help and picked the rice stalks. She winnowed enough rice for her step-mother and step-sisters' dinner.

She ran home with the rice and presented the basket full to the brim to her step-mother. Her step-mother took the basket and threw the rice on the terrace. "Foolish girl," said the step-mother, "See what you made me do? You made me lose my grip on the basket; now pick up all that rice!!" Little Pear Blossom saw that it was quite a lot of rice, and she knew she would not be done in time to go to the feast.

Quietly she said aloud, "Oh, how am I going to pick-up all this rice in time to go to the feast?" Just then, her friends the birds came and quickly picked up the rice for her. But, alas, it was getting late. She did not think she could make it to the feast. She decided she might be able to make it to the feast if she took the short cut near the stream nearby. So, she put on a light, yellow hanbok that she had been keeping for best wear and borrowed her step-sisters golden sandals—that were actually hers to begin with.

As she was walking along its banks, she heard a great thundering of horses' hoofs. She looked up and saw the banner of the prince himself. As she bowed down to the prince and his entourage, as she was told to do, she slipped and fell into the stream. She was so ashamed that she hid among the reeds till the prince rode on. As she left the stream, dripping wet, she realized she lost her step-sister's sandal that she borrowed for the trip to the feast. Oh no, she thought, she will be in worse trouble since she borrowed the sandals without permission.

Well, unbeknownst to Pear Blossom one of prince's men found the shoe. He brought to the prince who had actually seen Little Pear Blossom before she hit among the reeds. He thought she was beautiful, and sorry that he could not find her. He decided he would find the girl whose golden sandal would match the one his man found. And, he sent out a great proclamation to let the whole village know he was looking for the beautiful girl of the stream.

Little Pear Blossom had hidden the other sandal before her step-sister noticed that they were missing. When the prince came to look for the matching sandal, Pear Blossom was locked away in the barn. But, her faithful friends, the animals—especially the crickets and birds, made such a din, that the prince's man went to check on the barn. He opened the hasp and found the faithful dog had the same golden sandal—the match to the one found-- in his mouth, and he gave it to the man. When the prince saw it, he demanded that whoever was in the barn come out at once. Out came Pear Blossom and, right away, the prince remembered her from the stream. He asked, "Are these the golden sandals you were wearing when I rode by?" Little Pear Blossom timidly nodded her head with a yes. "Then come away with me," he said, "because I have been in love you at first sight. I can tell you are a great one and will rule this land with me."

The step-mother and step-sisters were so upset. "Who will look after us now?" demanded the step-mother. The prince looked at her and said, "Just be happy I don't make you live in the barn as you did lovely Pear Blossom!!" With that the step-mother began to scream and throw such a temper tantrum that she went up in a puff of smoke! The step-sisters kept quiet after that and wished Pear Blossom happiness. Pear Blossom looked at them and kindly told them they can live their lives in her home. Then she left with the prince to live with him in his palace.

Kindness, even to animals and those who are mean to you, does pay off.

Motifs for Cautionary Tales

Motifs	La Illarona	Babes in the Woods	Korean Cinderella
Threatened Children	X	X	X
False Parent	X		X
Supernatural Helpers	X		X
Supernatural			X

Advisary			
Magic Words, Potion, or Object	X		X
Magical Transformation	X		X
Testing of Main Character	X		X
Perilous Journey	X	X	X
Threatened Kingdom			
Kindness Rewarded			X
Evil Punished	X		X
Helpful or Grateful Animal		X	X
Stupid Ogre			X
Rescued Maiden			
Deception or Disguise	X		X

Source "Common Folktale Motifs," Elements of Literature, Fourth Course, 1993.

Symbols and Meanings in Cautionary Tales

Symbol	Meaning	La Illarona	Babes in the Woods	Korean Cinderella
Animals	Various animals are connected with pri-	Human animals-dangers	Robin-funeral	Frog-water Crickets-good luck Birds-fire Ox-cosmic forces

	mal waters: Fire and Cosmic Forces			
Color	Most universal of all types of symbolism	Green-spanning two groups	Red-assimilation	Gold/Yellow/White-intensity, activity, and light
Fire	Vital heat-need for life	Only darkness of the woods	Moon went down Stars gave no light	Life is abundant with eternal hope
Fruit	Equivalent to an egg-center of fruit Represents origin	No fruit-antithesis of motherhood	Strawberry leaves-seeds are external/use of leaves	Pear Blossom-promise of fertility
Humans	Terrible Mother-death Pieta-form of god of destiny	Angry, vulture mother preying on little children	Hinted pieta-like mother—crying for her lost babies	True mother-pieta Step-mother-preying, unkind

Source *The Uses of Enchantment: The Meaning and Importance of Fairy Tales,* 1976.

SKILLS for the Teaching Unit[20]

Knowledge

- Knowledge of dates, events, places
- Knowledge of major ideas
- Master of subject matter

Questions and Cues:

List	Show	Name
Tell	When	Collect
Quote	Who	Tabulate
Define	Describe	Examine

Questions:

- What happened after…?
- How many…?
- Who was it that…?
- Describe what happened…?
- Who spoke to…?
- Can you tell me who…?
- What is…?
- What is true…?
- Find the meaning of…?

Activities:

- List the main characteristics for each main character.
- Arrange a scrambled story pictures in sequential order.

---

[20] From Pamela Angelle Lecture

- Recall details about the setting.

Comprehension Level

- Interpretation of facts, comparison and contrast
- Order, group and infer causes
- Predict consequences
- Understanding information
- Grasping meaning
- Translation of knowledge into new context

Questions and Cues:

Explain	Predict	Summarize
Interpret	Restate	Extend
Outline	Compare	Contrast
Discuss	Describe	Distinguish

Questions:

- Can you write in your own words…?
- Can you provide a definition for…?
- Who do you think…?
- What was the main idea…?
- Can you provide an example of…?
- What differences exist between…?
- What do you think could have happened afterwards…?

Activities:

- Interpret pictures of scenes from the chapter.

- Explain selected ideas or parts of the story in your own words.
- Write a sentence explaining what happened before and after the event.
- Predict what could happen next.
- Explain how the main character felt at the beginning, middle, and end of the story.

Application

- Use information
- Use methods, concepts, theories in new situations
- Solve problems using required skills

Questions and cues:

Apply	Show	Change
Illustrate	Relate	Complete
Modify	Calculate	Examine
Solve	Classify	Demonstrate

Questions:

- Do you know another instance when…?
- Could this have happened…?
- What factors would change if…?
- What questions would you ask of…?
- Would this information be useful if you had a…?
- Can you apply the method to some experience of your own…?

Activities:

- Classify the character in the story as human, animal, or thing.
- Think of a situation that occurred here and write how you have handled it differently.
- Give examples that have the same problems.

Analysis

- Seeing patterns
- Organization of part
- Recognition of hidden meanings
- Identification of components

Questions and cues:

Analyze	Connect	Compare
Separate	Classify	Select
Order	Arrange	Infer
Explain	Divide	Debate

Questions:

- Which event could not have happened?
- If…happened, how might this have turned out?
- How was this similar to…?
- What are other outcomes?
- How is…similar to…?
- What are some of the problems of…?
- What was the problem with…?
- What are some of the motives behind…?

Activities:

- Identify general characteristics-main or implied-of…
- Distinguish what could happen from what could hot happen in this…?
- Differentiate fact from opinion?
- Compare and contrast two characters.

Synthesis

- Generalize from facts given
- Relate knowledge from several areas
- Predict, draw conclusions
- Use old ideas to create new ones

Questions and cues:

- What is a possible solution to…?
- What would happen if…?

Activities:

- Create a story from just the title before the story is read.
- Advertise an event from the story.
- Write a diary entry from the character.
- Create an original character and weave him/her into the existing story.

Evaluation

- Recognize subjectivity

- Verify value of story moral
- Make choices base on reasoned arguments

Questions and cues:

Assess	Test	Select
Decide	Measure	Judge
Rank	Recommend	Support
Grade	Convince	Conclude

Activities:

- Decide which character in the story you would like to spend time with and tell why.
- Judge whether or not the character should have acted as he/she did.
- Decide if the story really could have happened and justify why.

Writing from Sources
Using Evidence To:
- Inform
- Make arguments
- Respond to ideas, events, facts and arguments presented in the text

Narrative
- Conveys experience i.e. fictional stories, memoirs, anecdotes, autobiographies

Academic Vocabulary

- Tier One: everyday speech. This would be the modality for the folk tale and the fairy tale.

Common Core ELA Literacy

- Introduce a topic; organize ideas, concepts, and information, using strategies such as definition, classification, comparison/contrast, and cause/effect; include formatting (e.g., headings), graphics (e.g., charts, tables), and multimedia when useful to aiding comprehension.

- Use appropriate transitions to clarify the relationships among ideas and concepts.

- Write narratives to develop real or imagined experiences or events using effective technique, relevant descriptive details, and well-structured event sequences.

- Engage and orient the reader by establishing a context and introducing a narrator and/or characters; organize an event sequence that unfolds naturally and logically.

- Use narrative techniques, such as dialogue, pacing, and description, to develop experiences, events, and/or characters.

- Use a variety of transition words, phrases, and clauses to convey sequence and signal shifts from one time frame or setting to another.

- Use precise words and phrases, relevant descriptive details, and sensory language to convey experiences and events.

- Provide a conclusion that follows from the narrated experiences or events.

Production and Distribution of Writing

- Produce clear and coherent writing in which the development, organization, and style are appropriate to task, purpose, and audience. (Grade-specific expectations for writing types are defined in standards 1–3 above.)
- With some guidance and support from peers and adults, develop and strengthen writing as needed by planning, revising, editing, rewriting, or trying a new approach.
- Use technology, including the Internet, to produce and publish writing as well as to interact and collaborate with others; demonstrate sufficient command of keyboarding skills to type a minimum of three pages in a single sitting.

Resources

- Angelle, Pamela. Lecture. ELA Workshop #3: Reading Comprehension, 9 October 2003.
- Bettelheim, Bruno. *The Uses of Enchantment: The Meaning and Importance of Fairy Tales.* New York: Knopf, 1976.
- Cirlot, Juan E. *A Dictionary of Symbols.* New York: Philosophical P., 1983.
- Climo, Shirley. *The Korean Cinderella.* Mexico: Harper Collins, 1993.

- *Elements of Literature: Fourth Course.* Robert Anderson, ed. Dallas: Holt, Rhinehart, and Winston, Inc./Harcourt, Brace, Jovanovich, 1993.

- Neuner, Tomasa Gonsales. "La Illarona: An Oral Tale. 12 June 1999.

- Reed, Carrie Terhune. "Poor Babes in the Woods." A Lullaby. 12 April 1963.

- Raskin, Joseph and Edith. Tales Our Settlers Told. New York: Lothrop, Lee, and Shepard. 1971.

- Shedlock, Marie L. *The Art of the Story-Teller.* Toronto: Dover Publications, Inc. 1971.

- Warner, Marina From the Beast to the Blond: On Fairy Tales and Their Tellers. New York: Farrar, Straus, and Giroux, 1995.

About the author

Christine Neuner has 40 years teaching experience and is presently an adjunct professor at Northwestern State University of Louisiana. She has a doctorate in education leadership from the University of the Cumberlands, Kentucky. Her dissertation topic is Teaching Adult Learners: An Assessment of Instructional Practices in Two- and Four-Year Colleges in Select Southeastern States; she is also published in several academic journals and chapbooks. She lives in New Iberia, Louisiana, with her husband David with whom she enjoys travelling the U.S. and Europe. They have two children and four grandchildren. Contact information: chrisneuner71@gmail.com.

Carrie Longo Palmesano

Making Waves: Freedom Writer Methodology

Navigating the murky waters of teen hood can be especially painful for urban teens who have experienced multiple taxing ordeals: loss, addiction, violence, abuse, rape and rejection. Some teens feel like they are drowning in their own lives, swirling in deep oceans of grief without a sense of self or safety. Freedom Writer Methodology not only keeps teens afloat, but also provides a vessel to self-discovery and community. A Freedom Writer classroom endows introspection, personal empowerment, and a broadening world vision to develop empathy for others.

Writing forces a person to reflect on one's place in the world. Writing one's personal story allows a person to delve deep into the interior of one's soul, which leads to a healing process of self-discovery. This time of introspection validates the individual's struggles and develops problem solving skills to write one's own continuing story with a positive vision for the future. Keeping a Freedom Writer journal encourages a young person to examine his or her life on this level. The process helps teen writers realize that their stories matter. They matter. While some choose to keep their stories anonymous while sharing, revealing their stories to peers in a safe classroom setting requires immense courage. This results in personal empowerment of both claiming one's identity and story and sharing it.

Writing one's story puts the writer in control. The writer not only deals with life's challenges, but also determines the attitude with which he or she faces those obstacles. Making oneself the protagonist of one's own story is so powerful. Instead of life just happening to an individual, taking pen into hand affords the writer control over life's circumstances. They become the hero of their own story, more likely to see how personal decisions determine future fate and success. Sharing initially makes the writer feel vulnerable; however, soon receiving validation and positive feedback from one's peers and teacher fosters personal growth and deepens a sense of self and community. Those shaky teen voices and trembling hands holding their diaries lead to confident embraces with newfound friends. They develop a profound sense of respect for each other through this process, learning of each other's struggles and tragedies. I've witnessed Freedom Writers classes gather for group hugs, meet after school together with their teacher to share writing or even just hang out. Last year's classes still meet for periodic reunions with their teacher, watching movies together and sharing snacks. They forged a bond so strong through their writing, and they do not want to lose that sense of community. But coming to terms with one's personal journey only encompasses a portion of the Freedom Writer experience. One must also learn of worldwide struggle to further personal growth.

The personal journey of introspection, while incredibly vital and powerful, would be ultimately selfish if not coupled with an external understanding of the world and resulting action from what one learns. Freedom Writer Methodology purposefully exposes youth to oppressive circumstances in world history and current events to develop empathic humans who will speak up with moral conviction and work against injustice. So often a teen's world is encapsulated into a shrunken microcosm of society: high school, social group, and family. In order to transcend this myopic paradigm, it is imperative to expose teens to other world circumstances. Freedom Writer curriculum includes Holocaust literature, study of genocide, civil rights, and war. Our students learn to look beyond their realities to grasp what human struggle looks like elsewhere. My students had learned a great deal about the Holocaust, starting in grade school, but they were absolutely shocked to learn of the genocide in Rwanda. We watched *Hotel Rwanda*, read Paul Rusesabagina's book *An Ordinary Man*, and heard testimony from his son, Tresor, who visited our school. Learning of such inhumane atrocities fosters a deep respect for the precious value of life. It also puts one's own struggles into perspective. My students gained a better understanding of what great moral conviction looks like in action. Seeing Paul make those choices to risk his own life in order to save many lives serves as a concrete example of courage in the face of overwhelming adversity. His deep sense of humility also reminds them that anyone can be a hero. My hope for my students includes them making waves in life, being those ripples of change when faced with oppression. Freedom Writer Methodology forges this path for them in a manageable way that leaves impressionable lessons. These life lessons are invaluable, and coupled with introspective writing, help develop beautiful human beings who can now navigate life's tumultuous waters with grace, even more likely to extend a hand to pull another struggling soul aboard.

About the author

Carrie Palmesano teaches English at Omaha South High Magnet. She has taught in Omaha Public Schools in Nebraska for twenty years. She serves as the Vice President of the Omaha Freedom Writers Foundation, a nonprofit that supports students and teachers. She and her husband have three children.

Sue Burdett Robinson

Equity vs. Equality: What Can You Do To Level the Playing Field?

Abstract

Lev Vygotsky, Russian psychologist posited that social and cultural forces greatly impacted cognitive development. He believed that people's social and cultural environments served as the "filters" with which they assessed and evaluated people, events, situations, and navigated or explored their life spaces. A group of young people, who became known as the Freedom Writers (FW), from Woodrow Wilson High School in Long Beach, California, in the 1990s, developed their 'cognitive filter' from neighborhoods shaped by violence, drugs, death, and mistrust. A quality education was considered to be learning survival skills on the streets not academics in the classroom. Yet, all 150 of the original Freedom Writers graduated high school, most obtained a college degree, many are now educators in the classrooms, many are motivational speakers, and they are successful in their chosen fields. This article will address the defining forces that altered the 'cognitive filter' of those lost students that drove them to succeed and how educators can effectively be that cultural force to their students today.

Introduction

Lev Vygotsky, Russian psychologist, broadened Jean Piaget's work on the stages of cognitive development by positing that social and cultural forces greatly impacted cognitive development. He believed that people's social and cultural environments served as the "filters" with which they assessed and evaluated people, events, situations, and navigated or explored their life spaces. Social and cultural forces are the foundation of worldviews, values and beliefs. Those psychological tools facilitate and promote growth, knowledge and learning.

Another concept Vygotsky introduced to psychology and education was scaffolding. Scaffolding is defined as "Supported learning during its early phases through such techniques as demonstrating how tasks should be accomplished, giving hints to the correct solution to a problem or answer to a question, and providing leading questions. As students become more capable of working independently, these supports are withdrawn" (Snowman & McCown, 2015, p. 633.) In other words, if an educator effectively guides students through difficult concepts, questions or problems, the students will develop the skills to solve future problems independently...even beyond what they thought, believed, or were told they could do. Being able to accomplish beyond what they believed they could do is surpassing the zone of proximal development according to Vygotsky.

How does an educator effectively scaffold and lead students beyond the zone of proximal development? A four-component model has been theorized to include (1) model desired academic behaviors, (2) create a dialogue with the student, (3) practice, (4) confirmation (Snowman & McCown, 2015). Some students may not have demonstrated 'desired academic behavior' because they were not aware of what that meant; they believed they did not have the capacity to do so; parents or teachers did not believe they had the capacity to do so, therefore, the students projected that attitude. Scaffolding, as described in the previous paragraph, fosters desired academic behaviors. Promoting dialogue with students delivers the message that the education process is a collaborative effort, a relationship that stimulates brainstorming and free-thinking. Practice nurtures self-confidence and a secure preparedness to attempt even the impossible or the unimaginable. Confirmation translates into advocacy, encouragement, support, affirmation and trust.

I propose that a fifth component should be added to the model that combines the core conditions essential for effective [therapeutic] change to take place according to Carl Rogers, American humanistic psychologist (James & Gilliland, 2003.) The core conditions are unconditional positive regard, empathy and congruence/genuineness. According to Dr. Rogers, if an environment is created that allows patients/clients [or students] to believe they are truly being heard and to feel free to express themselves without fear of negative consequences, they are able to develop skills for solving or dealing with the challenges of life, and feel secure enough to explore possibilities beyond their own dreams or expectations.

The students, who later would become known as the Freedom Writers, of Woodrow Wilson High School in Long Beach, California in the 1990s were a classic example of Vygotsky's theory on the cultural impact of learning. They were learned in the ways of the streets and in survival as they navigated their life spaces. Their perspective of an education and what all that entails was on the opposite end of the academic continuum from what the expectations of the teachers at Wilson High. The lives of those students would change drastically when they were assigned Freshman English in Room 203 with Erin

Gruwell. Ms. Gruwell (Ms. G as she is still lovingly called) epitomized Vygotsky's theory. By appreciating her students' life space and focusing on their strengths instead of their perceived weaknesses, Ms. G confirmed that ALL young people CAN surpass the zone of proximal development if a teacher effectively leads the students in the learning process, and, according to Rogers, creates a safe environment that fosters freedom of expression and creativity.

Meritocracy and a Level Playing Field

Society in the United States promotes the concept of meritocracy; anyone who wishes to succeed can, if he/she works hard enough. Conversely, if the individual does not succeed, he/she did not make a concerted effort based on the constitutional right of equality afforded to him/her. Is that a fair statement?

Meritocracy also relies on an egalitarian society that promises a level playing field for all. It is based solely on personal skill, work ethic, and abilities without consideration of external factors. External factors, both past and present, play a significant role in how an individual views self, others and the outside world. The extrinsic factors incorporate the physical environment (life's necessities) as well as the actions of the people who cross his/her path. Oppression, marginalization, discrimination, socioeconomic status, etc., are not taken into consideration as prohibitive elements to advancement, achievement, or success. Does everyone have equitable exposure to resources and opportunities? In the world of education or even in the game of life, do all students/people have a level playing field? It is my contention that they do not.

For example, students in the wealthier school districts are given IPads or laptops, have well stocked libraries, the best sports and fitness facilities, updated classrooms and technology, exposure to cultural experiences through guest speakers or field trips, etc. For the most part, the students will likely have educated parents who encourage and support their pursuit of education and academic success. The poorer school districts have deficient equipment, inadequate facilities, and piteous opportunities of exposure to cultural experiences that promote students' maximum potential for growth and learning. Often times, there is no encouragement or support in the students' educational pursuits due to the family members' lack of understanding of the world of academia, family dynamics or dysfunctional, even toxic, environmental influences. Perhaps, the students are overlooked by the very institution whose responsibility it is to educate them. Perhaps, the administration, or even the teachers, considered them a 'lost cause' due to past behaviors or poor grades. That is basically the educational environment at Wilson High for the Freedom Writers in the 1990s. Yet, all 150 of the original Freedom Writers graduated high school, most obtained a college degree, many are now educators in the classrooms, many are motivational speakers, and they are successful in their chosen fields. What and/or who leveled the playing field for them?

Equity vs. Equality

As stated previously, the United States Constitution upholds the fundamental tenet of equality for all, regardless of race, creed, religion, etc. Equality, by definition, promotes the same treatment for people in a society or community regardless of social group. SES and other external factors are not considered. Take into consideration that a Math teacher is teaching the concept of fractions to elementary students. A fair and equality minded teacher will spend exactly 3 minutes with each student individually. Will equal time given be sufficient or ensure that every student has mastered the concept?

On the other hand, equity promotes treatment based on needs. An equitable Math teacher teaching the concepts of fractions will check with each student individually to ensure mastery of the concept; however, he/she allots more one-on-one instructional time for the students who require greater understanding in order to master the lesson and less one-on-one instructional time for those who have demonstrated complete understanding of the lesson.

I have used a Freedom Writer activity to demonstrate the idea that equity is vital in a world of social diversity (a concept of awareness and acceptance of the differences among people). The circumstances or social and cultural forces of the students often precipitate an uneven playing field regarding educational opportunities, preparedness for college, and/or in achieving professional success. More importantly, the activity focuses on the responsibilities that educators have to their students that go well beyond classroom instruction.

The Line Game

I begin the activity with the disclaimer that none of the questions that I ask are meant to cause the participants distress, and that I (a licensed therapist) am available for counseling following the activity if needed. Anything that is disclosed during the demonstration is held in professional confidence. The purpose and the outcome of the demonstration can only be validated through the honest participation from those in attendance. I assure the participants that the outcome will be reflected in a positive light. (I have used this activity with Masters level students and with professional educators and therapists at national and international conferences.)

The activity is held in a room with desks/chairs lined against the walls and out of the way. There is a taped line in the middle of the floor. All participants begin the activity standing on the line facing in the same direction. The participants are instructed to take one step forward or one step backward in accordance with their response to the following questions:

1. If your ancestors were forced to come to the USA (or their respective country) not by choice, take one step back.
2. If your primary ethnic identify is American (or their respective country) take one step forward.
3. If you were ever called names because of your race, class, ethnicity, gender, disability or sexual orientation, take one step back.
4. If you were ever ashamed or embarrassed of your clothes, house, car, etc., take one step back.
5. If your parents were professionals: doctors, lawyers, etc., take one step forward.
6. If you were reared in an area where there was prostitution, drug activity, etc., take one step back.

7.   If you ever tried to change your appearance, mannerisms, or behavior to avoid being judged or ridiculed, take one step back.

8.   If you studied the culture of your ancestor in elementary school, take one step forward.

9.   If you went to a school speaking a language other than English, take one step back.

10.   If there were more than 50 books in your house when you were growing up, take one step forward.

11.   If you ever had to skip a meal or were hungry because there was not enough money to buy food when you were growing up, take one step back.

12.   If you were taken to art galleries or plays by your parents, take one step forward.

13.   If one of your parents were unemployed or laid off, not by choice, take one step back.

14.   If your family ever had to move because they could not afford the rent, take one step back.

15.   If you were regularly told that you were beautiful/handsome, smart, and capable by your parents, take one step forward.

16.   If you were ever discouraged from academics or jobs because of race, class, ethnicity, gender, disability or sexual orientation, take one step back.

17.   If you were encouraged to attend college by your parents, take one step forward.

18.   If you have more than three closes relatives (e.g. parents, uncles, aunts, grandparents) who were graduated from college, take one step forward.

19.   If you were reared in a single parent home, take one step back.

20.   If your family owned the home where you grew up, take one step forward.

21.   If you often saw members of your race, ethnic group, gender, disability or sexual orientation portrayed on television in degrading roles, take one step back.

22.   If you were ever offered a good job because of your association with a friend or family member, take one step forward.

23.   If you feel you were ever denied employment because of your race, ethnicity, gender, disability or sexual orientation, take one step back.

24.   If you were paid less, treated unfairly because of race, ethnicity, gender, disability or sexual orientation, take one step back.

25.   If you had to rely on public transportation, take one step back.

26.   If you were ever stopped or questioned by police based on race, ethnicity, gender, disability or sexual orientation, take one step back.

27.   If you were ever afraid of violence because of your race, ethnicity, gender, disability or sexual orientation, take one step back.

28.   If you were generally able to avoid places that were dangerous, take one step forward.

29.   If you were ever uncomfortable about a joke related to your race, ethnicity, gender, disability or sexual orientation but felt unsafe to confront the situation take one step back.

30.   If you were ever the victim of violence related to your race, ethnicity, gender, disability or sexual orientation, take one step back.

31.   If your parents did not grow up in the U.S. (or their respective country), take one step back.

32.   If you were able to worship as you wish without fear or opposition, take one step forward.

33.   If you ever felt uncomfortable about, ashamed of, or afraid about your race, ethnicity, gender, disability or sexual orientation, take one step back.

34.   You have or have not altered your appearance in some significant way to fit in, take one step back.

35.   You generally have relatively easy physical access to buildings, take one step forward.

36.   If you have gone to meetings of organizations where you felt isolated, outnumbered, or out of place, take one step back.

37.   If anyone in your family needed medical care and were not financially able to go, take one step back.

Processing:

I have all the participants to make note of their position relative to the beginning line AND as compared to the other participants. Then, they are asked to be seated.

Reflection of the activity either on paper or through oral discussion:

- What was your position relative to your class-mates/colleagues?

- How did the exercise make you feel?
- What were your thoughts as you did the exercise?
- What have you learned from the experience?
- Was there anything that you disagreed with?
- How can you use this information/experience as professionals/educators in the future?

Everyone who participated… (If students, they are in a Masters level program in higher education; if an educated professional, they have achieved success and are respected in their chosen fields.) …in spite of his/her circumstances and where they began their life's journey. Especially, acknowledge those participants who are behind the line and maybe even isolated from most of the other participants. In spite of whatever the circumstances, they have achieved success…someone and/or something HAD to make a difference and impacted the choices they made.

All began on the same line, an even/level playing field as he/she rested in his/her crib in the nursery at the hospital following his/her entrance into the world. However, it is when each one left that world and entered his/her own personal space that life's circumstances started impacting his/her life. As stated earlier, the extrinsic factors played a significant role in how he/she viewed himself/herself, others and the outside world. Intrinsic factors such as sense of self, motivation, strength and resilience may have laid dormant and undiscovered for years until someone and/or some event encouraged, supported, or instilled a determination and drive in each of him/her to succeed in spite of circumstances.

It is imperative when working with students (ALL students) that teachers/advocates appreciate the quality world/life space of each student or the challenges each face outside the confines of the classroom, and not just focus on class assignments, curriculum, and standardized tests. Social justice and advocacy demand that educators be proactive and not reactive. All scholars are called upon to be THAT someone who is the voice for the voiceless and hope for the hopeless, those who are inhibited by life's circumstances, and to empower those who are overlooked by the ideation of meritocracy and to level the playing field for all.

Summary

One of the objectives of this article/activity was to demonstrate how important equitable instruction, resources and opportunities are to all students. With that comes acceptance that not all people have a level playing field and that societal view of meritocracy can be achieved if equity is practiced. Another objective was to assess why equity is necessary, as represented in the stories of the Freedom Writers, through understanding the social and cultural forces that impact cognitive development as posited by Vygotsky. The most salient objective was to demonstrate how an educator through scaffolding, unconditional positive regard, empathy, congruence, and by creating a space of freedom, safety and affirmation (according to Rogers) WILL promote growth, learning, achievement, success, self-esteem, and pride as seen in Room 203 at Woodrow Wilson High School in Long Beach, California, in the 1990s. Thank you Ms. G for being a role model of acceptance, tolerance, and advocacy for the

Freedom Writers, yesterday and today, and for educators today all over the world.

*****

Between Teacher and Child
by Haim Ginott

I have come to a frightening conclusion.
I AM the decisive element in the classroom.
It is my personal approach that creates the climate.
It is my daily mood that makes the weather.
As a teacher, I possess tremendous power to make a child's life miserable or joyous.
I can be a tool of torture or an instrument of inspiration.
I can humiliate or humor, hurt, or heal.
In all situations, it is my response that decides whether a crisis will be escalated or de-escalated, and a child humanized or dehumanized.

*****

References

- Hays, D.G., & Erford, B.T. (2010). *Developing multicultural counseling competence: A systems approach.* Upper River Saddle, NJ: Pearson Education, Inc.
- James, R.K., & Gilliland, B.E. (2003). *Counseling & psychotherapy.* (5th ed.). Allyn and Bacon: Boston.
- McAuliffe, G., & Associates. (2013). *Culturally alert counseling. A comprehensive introduction.* (2nd ed.). Thousand Oaks, CA: Sage Publications, Inc.
- Snowman, J., & McCown, R. (2015). *Psychology applied to teaching.* (14th ed.) Wadsworth, Cengage Learning: Belmont, CA.

About the Author:

Sue Burdett Robinson, PhD, LPC-S, NCC, is a professor in a Masters Counseling program at a small liberal arts university in West Texas, USA. She is also a licensed therapist, a licensed supervisor of counseling interns, a certified teacher, and a certified school counselor. Dr. Sue enjoys traveling and presenting at conferences. She is heavily involved with efforts to promote growth and empower children/youth in her community. She serves as Vice President on the Board of the Boys/Girls Club and is proud to be a Freedom Writer Educator, which is part of a global movement to advocate for students "at risk" and promote social justice.

Torbjørn Ydegaard

Karl Popper and Hannah Arendt
– two interpretations on education

Hannah Arendt and Karl Popper were among the most influential philosophers of last the century – they both had a Jewish background, both were native German speakers and both had to flee the Nazi-regime. Hannah Arendt was German and ended up in the USA while Karl Popper was Austrian and via New Zealand ended up in England.

Different in their thinking as they are I choose to present them here in the same paper mainly because of what they share in relation to the Freedom Writers methodology:

- Their Jewish background
- Their relationship to Holocaust
- Their strong pro-democratic attitude
- Their work of bridge-building between continental European and Anglo-Saxon philosophy
- Their ideas about education, teaching and learning – which might not be central issues for none of them, but, I think, of great relevance for an understanding of the Freedom Writers methods.

My point is not that the Freedom Writers methodology is consciously based on either Hannah Arendt or Karl Popper – it is not! My point is only that I can reflect on and give perspectives to an understanding of the methodology by looking at it through the glasses of the two philosophers.

Due to what I want to focus on and concepts I want to bring forward, I will, not so very gentleman-like, start with Karl Popper and leave Hannah Arendt for the last part of my essay.

Karl Popper

Karl Popper was born into a wealthy and educated family of Jewish decent in Vienna in 1902. He grew up in a house filled with books and music. Summer holidays were spent in the Alps along with the sister of Sigmund Freud. In the aftermath of the collapse of the Austrian-Hungarian Empire in 1918 he had a short flirt with Marxism and he was deeply involved in social work. Teaching and studying toke over his time, and in 1934 he published *The Logic of Scientific Discovery* in which he actually 'killed' *positivism* and *induction* as ways of realization – which again led to a strong theory of learning through critical thinking, or critical rationalism as it is called.

Popper had to leave Austria in 1937 due to the growing threat of Nazism. He settled in New Zealand, where he stayed during World War II. Here he wrote two books as his contribution to the war against Nazism: *The Open Society and Its Enemies* and *The Poverty of Historicism*. They deal with ideologies leading to totalitarianism and they break with the idea of a 'natural' development of societies. Societies are not, Popper says, formed by a scientific detectable formula, as was the idea of for example Marx' *historical materialism*. On the contrary, we form our societies through our actions – therefore we have to realize that...

…instead of posing as prophets we must become the makers of our fate. We must learn to do things as well as we can, and to look out for our mistakes.

(Popper 1945/1973, vol. II: 280)

As makers of our fate, we not only take upon us the responsibility for ourselves and our families and friends. We have an obligation much larger than that – and very much in line with what we will see in Hannah Arendt's distinction between the French and the American Revolution: An obligation to work as hard as possible to create a society open to everybody, especially wherever we find in-justice, poverty and misery – *the* obligation that lead teachers and social workers towards practical methods like the ones learned by Freedom Writers? However, our morale duties are not to make heaven on Earth, because it invariably produces hell:

It is our duty to help those who need our help; but it cannot be our duty to make others happy, since this does not depend on us, and since it would only too often mean intruding on the privacy of those towards whom we have such amiable intentions.

(Popper 1945/1973, vol. II: 237)

To Popper his political thinking can be boiled down to the search for *a sober combination of individualism and altruism* (Popper 1945/1973, vol. II: 275).

Popperian theory of learning

Popper dares to put any scientific method, any theory of learning and any method of problem-solving into a formula (which I call "Popper's learning formula"):

$$P1 \rightarrow TT \rightarrow EE \rightarrow P2$$

P1 is the original problem or wonder that sets the process in motion. The problem may be an actual, experienced problem. Often, at least in the institutionalized schooling, where content, as seen from the student's side, is more or less given from the outside, is the teacher left with the challenge of making the content 'problematic' for the student.

The problem is being addressed with a deductively developed, provisional theory: TT (tentative theory). The provisional theory is to be tested, that is by all means possible tried falsified, in the face of reality, or by the mind: EE (error elimination). There are three outcomes of these tests:

1. The theory is falsified.
2. The test detects errors that can be corrected before new encounters with reality.
3. The theory cannot be falsified and remains provisionally accepted. The theory is not proven ('verified' is not an option), but has so far passed all attempts to falsify it.

Learning according to Popper's learning formula comes when you critically confront your prior understanding and knowledge (one of the ingredients in Ms. G's so called 'secret sauce' for better teaching) with reality – as far as you can get a picture of the reality.

Based on the learning formula and the critical rationalism we can never talk about absolute knowledge in the Aristotelian tradition (the tradition of *episteme*), because we do not know when new theories or tests will falsify our knowledge. All we can is to accept non-falsified knowledge as contemporary valid knowledge (in Greek: *doxa*). Therefore, we cannot say that 'knowledge' is something absolute. We are much closer to the truth if we understand that we are always in the never-ending process of finding better alternatives. This is actually what is meant by the concept of 'critical thinking'. As Popper puts it:

> *The growth of knowledge – or the learning process – is not a repetitive or a cumulative process but one of error-elimination. It is Darwinian selection, rather than Lamarckian instruction.*
>
> (Popper 1979: 144)

Any test of this type leads to a new situation – and probably to new questions and new wonders. Thus ends the formula with P2. P2 is rarely a planned problem. In most cases, it will even be an unforeseen problem. In fact, every action creates risks for the unexpected. That is why Popper argues against the objective-based didactics[21] and in favor of processes with a focus on 'addressing the immediate misery' in order to minimize the risk of the unpredictable.

It also means that we as individuals have reached our current level of knowledge through repetitive movements through

---

[21] Also Hannah Arendt argues, as we shall see, against objectives-based didactics in her critique of late modernity – but for some very different reasons.

the learning formula. In fact this dynamic is set in motion at the time of birth:

> *All acquired knowledge, all learning, consists of the modification (possibly by rejection) of some form of knowledge, or disposition, which was there previously; and in the last instance, of inborn dispositions*
>
> (Popper 1979: 71)

We are born with expectations of being taken care of, of being feed and of being kept warm (a similar argument is found in the thinking of Piaget) and have right from the beginning to test these expectations in relation to reality. The tests lead to falsification, error elimination or confirmation and thence to new situations and new expectations. Life is thus a matter of repeated problem solving processes via the dynamics of the learning formula – or as the title of one of Popper's books says: *All Life is Problem-Solving*. However, to learn something new it is important that we are facing new problems. Repetition of the same problem does not contribute to further learning, only to make desired behavior a routine.

This is clearly seen in the example of the amoeba that is exposed to a hostile environment. The amoeba runs through its repertoire of options and if it finds a suitable behavior in relation to the environment, it performs this behavior and survives. By repeated exposure to the same hostile environment, the amoeba reacts in the same way each time, with the only difference that it will be faster and faster in finding the appropriate behavior. It therefore becomes quicker to find the solution. However, it is not learning; it is making the behavior a routine.

Repetition does not create anything new, but might 're-move' old habits:

Habits and practice only remove the meanderings in the course of the reaction – straighten it out. Nothing is thus created by repetition. The increasing promptness of a reaction should not be regarded as its gradual creation (natura facit saltus).

(Popper: *Die beiden Grundprobleme
der Erkenntnistheorie,*
quoted from Petersen 1985: 233)

To pedagogy this is important. It is through conscious challenges of students' expectations, that teachers enable students to learn.

Therefore, in the Freedom Writers movie Ms. Campbell is wrong when she says that *"you can't make someone want an education"*. Right though – you cannot force the learning process, but you can make students want answers to questions, problems and wonderings. And that forces the learning process – just as what happens in the Freedom Writer movie when Tito ask about Holocaust!

Popper is a mild constructivist. With a reference to Denis Phillips, professor emeritus at Stanford University, some figures of the learning landscape illustrate this:

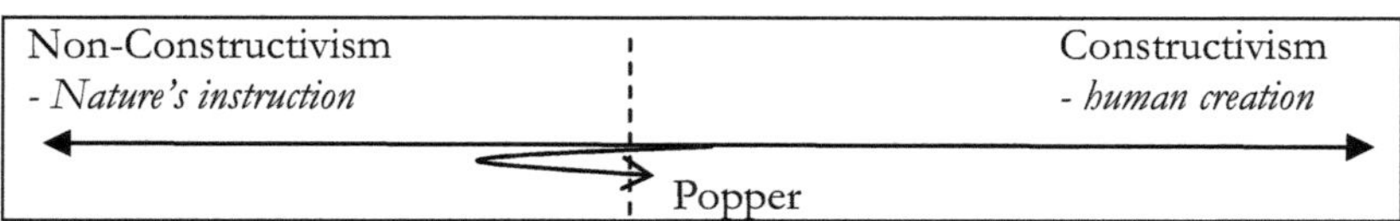

One of the axes through this landscape is stretching from non-constructivism to the constructivism, or from learning guided

112

by natures 'picture' to learning guided by human's creation. Popper ranks roughly in the middle of the scale, since TT of the learning-formula, the preliminary theory and derived hypothesis is deductively man-made and thus it is constructivism, while EE, error-elimination, happens in the encounter with 'nature' – the reality of its many 'realistic' facets, which also includes the societal realities, interpersonal relationships and the objective knowledge. *Man proposes, nature disposes,* such as Phillips quotes Popper saying. In this context Popper can be called a mild constructivist – or perhaps better: a balanced constructivist, because without this test of the individual constructed understanding there is a risk of significant error learning. Although knowledge is *doxa,* and therefore changeable and never absolute, there is still something that is more 'right' at the moment than anything else.

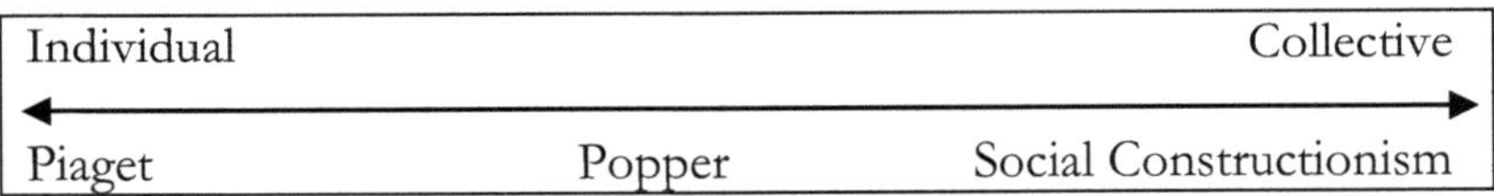

The second scale goes from learning as something purely individual to the purely collective learning. Learning theorists as Piaget and Vygotsky belong to the individual end of the scale; their focus is on the individual's cognitive development – albeit with respectively the biological/psychological and social context as explanatory factors. At the other end of the scale, you find the social constructionist theorists who see knowledge as something that, regardless of 'reality', is created jointly through communication. Here the language games that constitute communication are tools for social change, for example in organizations. The focus is on the relationships between people, not what happens inside humans. Also on this scale Popper, who with his learning-formula focuses on individual learning, but sees a qualification of this in the collective cooperative aspects of mutual criticism of ideas and theories, is balanced in the middle of the range.

When the students in the Freedom Writers movie are reading *The Diary of Anne Frank* and *Romeo and Juliet* they construct individual theories about the books and their meaning. However, the meaning of the books really gets to the students only when they relate them to the reality of their own lives – as we see Eva does when she storms into the classroom claiming that the death of Anne Frank *"ain't right"*, and asks *"when she dies, what does it say about me?"* This understanding and connection deepens further, when Marcus, in an act of collective cooperative and mutual criticism, relate Eva's anger to their gang-lives and to Miep Gies as his hero.

The concept of *Bildung*

In the German language area, which includes the Scandinavian languages too, we have a special concept for the process of becoming an educated person: *Bildung*. In lack of a similar English concept, I will stick to the German word. A direct translation is 'formation', which probably will be understood in a too instrumental way. As long as the content of the concept have to do with individual autonomy, it should be understood also in an English-speaking context.

The basic tenet of Popper's approach to *Bildung*, in which independence and the fight against tyranny is central, is without doubt the Kantian concept of authority taken from the article

What is Enlightenment?, which in many ways stands as the collecting end of the Enlightenment Era. The oft-quoted piece reads:

> *Enlightenment is man's emergence from his self-incurred immaturity. Immaturity is the inability to use one's own understanding without the guidance of another. This immaturity is self-incurred if its cause is not lack of understanding, but lack of resolution and courage to use it without the guidance of another. The motto of enlightenment is therefore: Sapere aude! Have courage to use your own understanding!*
>
> *Laziness and cowardice are the reasons why such a large proportion of men, even when nature has long emancipated them from alien guidance (naturaliter maiorennes), nevertheless gladly remain immature for life. For the same reasons, it is all too easy for others to set themselves up as their guardians. It is so convenient to be immature!*

(Kant 1784)

To Kant, man himself must take responsibility for his own life in the enlightened newfound freedom, and this responsibility unfolds through courageous use of reason. Autonomy is not merely God-given, it must be developed and trained – cultured, civilized and moralized – it must be willed by the individual. *Bildung* becomes Kant's answer to liberty's claim. Kant speaks of 'mind' and 'reason'. The mind is the instrumental rationality by which to recognize the immediate reality and the one you use technical. Reason is the reflexive rationality by which to seek metaphysics; assumptions and justifications for the immediate reality.

Popper talks about Kant's quote:

Kant is saying something very personal here. It is part of his own history. Brought up in near poverty, in the narrow outlook of Pietism — a severe German version of Puritanism — his own life was a story of emancipation through knowledge. In later years he used to look back with horror to what he called 'the slavery of childhood', his period of tutelage. One might well say that the dominant theme of his whole life was the struggle for spiritual freedom.

(Popper 1989: 177)

Bildung is to shake oneself free of the self-imposed immaturity with the use of enlightenment and knowledge. In this understanding of the *Bildung*-concept it must be linked to the individual, because only the individual can be a carrier of enlightenment, knowledge — and self-determination. You have, so to speak, to 'have something to wear your autonomy in', and this 'something' is the mind. The Self in this view is equipped to handle the authority of the individual, and should as such be socialized, trained and formed. The rational mind does not come by itself. However, it is not so much the extent or nature of the sense-related equipment that counts — it is far more the ability of the sense-based application of the given sense, that is the result of *Bildung* and what constitutes a free man in the western philosophical tradition.

The community that socialization has to adopt the child and the young into is and has always been changing. Therefore, the means for this socialization always changes. Through history there have always been discussions on the nature of these various instruments, because the choice of instruments affects the outcome — socialization. Essential in this context is the so-called 'educational paradox', as it unfolds in the modern and postmodern society. The paradox raises the question: "How raise and educate a child to independency?" The general answer is that upbringing – *Bildung* – whether it is in the primary or secondary socialization and based on an asymmetry between adult and child, in one way or another is to abolish itself, so that the child finally achieves the same degree of autonomy as the adults. This means that the child must acquire the Kantian authority in its own life.

The best example of *Bildung* in the Freedom Writers movie we find is in the scene where Eva is testifying in the court. Here she decides to emancipate herself from the tutelage of the gang. She has gone through the process of *Bildung* and has become a free, independent person – a person of *Bildung*.

Another beautiful example of *Bildung* is Miep Gies' words *"that I did what I have to do, because it was the right thing to do"*. This sentence is covered by the Hebrew concept *Mitzvah*, which is actually used as the brand for the Danish-Jewish Museum in Copenhagen that tells the story of how the Danish Jews, as the only Jewish community in Europe, were helped by ordinary Danes to escape to Sweden during WWII.

In Teaching Hope, (Gruwell 2009: 190), a teacher tells his class about a classmate that has been arrested for jumping an older couple, saying: *"Yeah, Shaud really screwed it up. The same kid most of you young boys looked up to failed himself, his family, and you by choosing to be a victim of the environment"*. This is an example of lack of *Bildung* where circumstance rules over autonomy[22].

---

22 In Europe, according to Hannah Arendt as we shall see, you don't choose to be a victim – you are forced to be one by the environment. The result is, that in Europe we 'take pity' on such a person, while in America he is (if he is lucky) given sympathy.

Shaud's behavior is contradicted by Renee Firestone in her Shoah Foundation-interview[23] when she says: *"I was a slave in my lifetime, but I survived. I have come to realize that <u>there are no excuses in life!</u>"* Besides understanding this in the perspective of Antonovsky's concept of salutogenesis, it is also an expression of autonomy where circumstance has no say.

The theory of *Bildung* is unfolded even more in the following on Popper's Matrix:

Popper's Matrix

An interesting feature of Popper is his detection of Plato's little propaganda ploy to get people to accept his theory of the ideal state, with its hierarchical and pyramidal structure, with all its totalitarian and repressive logics. And with the intention of putting Plato – himself – at the top of the pyramid as the philosopher king. For Plato leaders have to be the wisest – be it Plato himself, or *der Führer*, or the party's Central Committee, or...! Plato knew that people would not like this little detail. Thus, he writes:

> *The part exists for completeness' sake, but the whole does not exist for part's sake ... You are made for completeness' sake, and not the whole for your sake.*

(Plato 2014: 393)

In addition, so says Plato, whom that it will not conform to the collective altruism of the Republic is a selfish individualist. Thus did Plato and Western culture after him, make individualism

---

[23] https://www.youtube.com/watch?v=E2X7-NYbZE8

synonymous with selfishness and collectivism synonymous with altruism. As we often perceive it, even today. Schematic Plato's understanding is this:

Individualism	$\neq$	Collectivism
=		=
Egoism	$\neq$	Altruism

The state is in Plato's optics designed to create prosperity for the state itself. And it does this by...

> *...fitting people into a single unit, both using persuasion and power. It lets them share any advantage that each individual can contribute to the community. And it's actually the law that creates people with the right attitude to the state, not to unleash them, so that everyone can go their own way, but to use them to weld together the city.*
>
> (Plato 2013: 98)

This means that the state seeks to create a certain type of man – a human type that will be included in and be a part of the community without nourishing individual wishes – a human type to be all the opposite of Kant's autonomous individual. It is not *Bildung*, but totalitarianism! It becomes totalitarian pedagogy when the objectives is greater than the individual, when the care or welfare of the individual deprives it of its freedom and independency, and when uniformity in thinking slows the critical approach to the world – and thus the opportunity for the individual to self-improve its situation. Hannah Arendt, below, argues in the same lines.

The above table of the two binary pairs individualism and egoism, and collectivism and altruism, is, says Popper, only partly correct. Individualism and collectivism and egoism and altruism might well respectively be mutually opposed, but the equal signs between the individualism and egoism and between collectivism and altruism are not the only connections available. You can both imagine and in fact see examples of relations between, on one hand, individualism and altruism and on the other hand between collectivism and egoism. You can therefore also cross-combine the concepts. This will give you the basic pattern of what I have termed Popper's Matrix (Ydegaard: 130):

	Individualism	Collectivism
Egoism		
Altruism		

Popper's Matrix indicates that the primary human perception is either to see us as independent individual subjects or as individuals as part of and defined by a community. Secondarily, this basic view is supplemented with the variables egoism and altruism. Plato's two basic forms, the selfish individualistic and altruistic collective, are found in fields related to NW and SE. In addition, you will also find the combinations 'egoistic collective' and 'altruistic individualism' in the NE and SW respectively.

There are a number of basic attitudes and examples (I choose to make examples politically biased. It may be unfortunate, but since the arguments used in the case of *Bildung* refers to ideology and human understanding, I choose therefore to admit to this) linked to each of the fields in the matrix:

The collective-altruistic field is represented by the community, acting inclusive in relation to outsiders. Community is preceding the individual. This field is very much a carrier of the European self-understanding, the welfare state and the associated social human ideal, as we see below, in Arendt characteristic of the French Revolution. It is here we find the social democratic and socialist movements – movements and values that Plato gave a resemblance of humanity.

Opposite we find the individual-selfish field, as Plato endowed with a number of negative connotations. The field represents individuals who see themselves as lonely, subject to the jungle-law of the economy and often struggling against a society that is experienced collective-altruistic at the expense of individual freedoms. It is the individual before the community. This field largely carries the American self-understanding, the postmodern de-regulated economy and the associated self-managed human ideal. Political we find here the liberalist groups.

The NE-field represents the egoistic collective – the collective that closes in on itself and act for its own benefit. The community is preceding the subject and is in contrast to other individuals and communities. Here we find the national populism that is so prevalent in Europe – and elsewhere in the world. Here we also find many Middle Eastern immigrant groups, for whom their original home state could not guarantee the individual's safety and rights and where the family has been the backbone, to which the individual must submit – most cruelly exemplified by the honor killing of daughters and sisters who want to marry by love and against the family's will. A less dramatic, but perhaps more urgent example is found in the difference in the behavior of relatives of hospitalized persons. The traditional Western behavior indicates an individualistic approach with few visitors at a time, with respect for fellow patients, that guests leave the room during treatments, and that information goes from hospital staff to patient. For many middle-eastern groups it is quite the opposite. The starting point is the selfish collectivism, with many visitors over long periods, without respect for the needs of fellow patients and insistence that information goes through the family of the patient. The behavior is contrary to the hospitals' ethical code, but since it simultaneously is perceived to support the patient, which indeed expects this behavior, it cannot simply be dismissed, but must be handled as the dilemma it is.

Contrary to this, at the massacre at Utøya in Norway 2011 it was the young people of immigrant origin, who by themselves or at the request of their parents, whom they managed to talk to on the phone, tried to take up the fight against the superior force, or at least help comrades. The ethnic Norwegians only looked for themselves. Interpreted into Popper's Matrix, one can say that the young people of immigrant origin still possessed some of the qualities of the collective-selfish field – namely the willingness actively to protect and take care of its own and actively to take a stand against a foreign enemy. The born Norwegians' reaction is hardly covered by the matrix, as the reaction probably stems from an upbringing based on conversation as conflict resolution means – but against automatic weapons in the hands of lunatics talk does not call, and then there is only panic left.

In the Freedom Writers movie, it seems obviously that the gang members all belong to the egoistic collective: They are initiated into the gangs through a *rites de passage* (the beating up), *they have to protect their own* as Eva is told over and over and they definitely see other people and groups or gangs as enemies.

The fourth field – the field of the altruistic individual – is what is perceived by the individual as both the basic unit and as a political goal, and at the same time recognizes the claim, whether it is religious ("You shall love your neighbor as yourself," Matt. 22.39) or moral, of responsibility for one's Next. Or as the Danish theologian and philosopher Knud E. Løgstrup so aptly characterizes it:

> *The individual never has to do with another person without holding something of this person's life in his hand. It can be very little, a passing mood, a gusto, you get to wilt, or as you wake, a loath deepened or abolished. But it can also be terrifying much so that it simply stands for the individual, if the other's life is successful or not.*
>
> (Løgstrup 1986: 25)

In many ways these words of Løgstrup seems to be the guiding lights in the actions and didactics taken by Erin in the movie, where her own marriage suffer but at the same time the student's lives become successful.

Bildung-wise, the altruistic claim gives the consequence that the individual in trust of the reciprocity of meeting must open up and disclose to the Other, not only in empty tolerance of the Other's presence but out of respect for the Other's outlook on life. As Løgstrup writes, in is also an educational *claim to*

Again: This is what I see unfolded in Erin's work – the students certainly got a broader horizon.

Altruism is not entirely altruistic; it also serves the individual through what Popper calls the paradox of freedom. The paradox of freedom is the desire to let the state limit one's own freedom in order to protect the remaining freedom and the freedom of other people – it is freedom from the liberalist anarchy. This makes the SW the liberal (as opposed to liberalist) field. *By a liberal I [mean] simply a man who values individual freedom and who is alive to the dangers inherent in all forms of power and authority* (Popper 1989: viii). Should there be a political color here, it must be the philosophical conservativism – with the suspicion, that today's conservative parties do not quite seem to live up to these initial positions.

Thinking in individually-altruistic lanes is probably more rational, seen in the broad perspective, than, for example, to think individually-selfish.

Research conducted by Michael Bang Petersen from Aarhus University shows that altruism is not just a nifty ideological idea, but also a rational evolutionarily acquired strategy that lies deep in the human gene pool. Altruism has been a survival strategy for humans, since we climbed down from the trees and started walking across the savannah. For only through mutual aid – reciprocal altruism – could single individuals survive and ensure the species' survival. This reciprocal altruism is also reflected in a number of animal species. But altruism is exactly reciprocal: we are, regardless of cultural background (and Petersen has specifically examined and compared attitudes in the

U.S. and Denmark), willing to share our resources with people who out of unfortunate reasons they do not have control over, ended up in an economic or social limbo. By contrast, we look with skepticism on welfare benefits to persons perceived as lazy:

> *…the deservingness heuristic is rooted in psychological categories that evolved over the course of human evolution to regulate small-scale exchanges of help. That is, beneath the real and substantial variation in individual perceptions of the effort of welfare recipients, a species-typical set of psychological categories exists in us all, motivating us to extract and respond to information about the effort of those in need of help.*
>
> (Petersen 2012)

Petersen's arguments support the claim of the altruistic human, maybe even so much that altruism is vindicated by biology and evolution, while egoism, as many has claimed as a predominant characteristic of man, is ideologically grounded?

In the movie, Eva's starting-point is the NE corner of the matrix, the selfish collective of the gangs. Nevertheless, through the acts of Erin and the wise words of Miep Gies she starts to doubt this ideology. Gradually she moves towards the SW, towards the altruistic individual, taking on her shoulders the responsibility of being a human individual. This culminates in the courtroom. By telling the truth, she not only denies her relations to the gangs and the NE of the matrix and places herself in the SE corner. She also starts a movement of trust in other people, based on the reciprocity of 'deservingness' – and the next day the Cambodian girl Cindy accept and return this trust.

Basically the didactics of the Freedom Writers are about helping the participants to move their attitudes towards the altruistic individual corner of the matrix. This indicates a fundamental belief in *Bildung* – in the autonomy of the individual combined with caretaking of those in need. In the movie, the starting point of the participants is the NE corner. However, the fundamental idea will work just as well with participants coming from NW (the rich, selfish kids of the suburbs?) or SE (the common European attitude?).

Hannah Arendt

Hannah Arendt (1906-1975) was raised in Königsberg (now Kaliningrad) in East-Prussia. In the 1920th she studied theology, philosophy and classical philology in Marburg, Heidelberg and Freiburg under teachers like Rudolf Bultmann, Martin Heidegger (with whom she is told to have had a love-affair) and Karl Jaspers. Here she met with various aspects of Christianity and existentialism that might have formed some of her later thoughts – for example that The New Testament could tell us about some basic conditions of the human life, that our relations with the material world defines us as individuals and that we actually are a part of our own environment, but also that we as individuals have to deliberate on whom we are and from where we come – that we can only develop as humans by communicating to other humans our own narratives.

In 1933, Arendt had to leave Germany. After living in France, she in 1941 escaped to the US where she lived until her death.

One of Hannah Arendt many books is *Eichmann in Jerusalem* from 1963. The book is an account of the trial against Adolf Eichmann, who organized the Holocaust. The most shocking for me by reading the book was not so much the account of the death of so many or the amount of logistic resources a war-torn Germany had to put into the extermination of the millions. No, the shocking effect came from reading about the administrative problems that Eichmann faced, and how he solved them by manipulating even the many Jewish societies of Europe. Without their assistance, it seems that Holocaust would never have reached its historical magnitude. Gregory Stanton later on has formulated the eight steps in a Holocaust, like what we have seen in Cambodia and Rwanda: Classification, symbolization, dehumanization, organization, polarization, preparation, extermination and denial. The parallel to street-gangs and their internal fights seems clear —what also Erin Gruwell saw in the film-scene were Tito's picture is disclosed. The way to prevent genocide – or the gang-war in the streets – is to prevent all classification and symbolization to flourish. Tolerance, promoted diversity and spirit of community, as practiced by The Freedom Writers methodology, is key concepts and actions to be taken here.

Reflections on Little Rock

In the aftermath of the incident in 1957 at Central High in Little Rock, Arkansas, where Elizabeth Eckford, a black girl, tried to enter the then all-white school and was met by a huge mob that cursed her away in a near lynch-atmosphere, Hannah Arendt wrote the essay *Reflections on Little Rock*. Due to the controversial content (*a landmine* it was called by Roger Berkowitz, Bard College) and Arendt's disagreement with the strategies of NAACP, it took about two years to get it printed.

I am in no position to judge on this controversy, but the philosophy behind Arendt's arguments is still worth a reflection as it might put also today's pedagogy into a broader perspective.

Arendt distinguishes between three spheres in which man is living his life; the private, the social and the political:

The private is the realm of the family. To a liberal thinker as Hannah Arendt *the private* is the place where everyone enjoys the freedom of living a life as he or she chooses. It is the place of retreat from the social and political life. It is also here you raise your children to the standards you yourself put up. As such, *the private* is the realm of the necessities of life – what Arendt calls *labor*.

The social is the public sphere where we act together with other people outside *the private*. In an open society, you are free to choose with whom you want to interact. It is also in this sphere we earn our living and produce our man-made material world. In *the social* we *work*.

The political is to Arendt the realm of protection – the protection of human and political rights. It is also the only level, to which Arendt applies *equity* among humans – we all have equal rights to vote for government, equal rights to be voted into office and we all stand equal in front of the law. *The political* belongs in this way to what Arendt calls *action*.

Public schools work in the triangle between *the private*, *the social* and *the political*. They are initiated and run by *the political* and is needed in modern societies, both due to the economy and due to the democracy. Still, in the eyes of Hannah Arendt, schools are also a challenge to *the private* to which the child belongs. To the child, on the other hand, the school is the first introduction into *the social*, into the interaction with other people – but lacking the free choice of whom to interact with.

The main problem to Hannah Arendt, when she is reflecting on Little Rock, occurs when *the political* impose practices (objective-based didactics) in the schools that goes beyond what is needed for economy and democracy (later she is actually narrowing this standpoint to cover only *Bildung*) – when schools are used as tools for solving main and unsolvable problems in *the social* as were the case in the conflict between Blacks and Whites in the South. In a state of affairs where laws in many States still prohibited mixed marriages – which to Hannah Arendt were a violation of the freedom of *the private*[24] – integrated schools were introduced by force as a mean to solve the conflict. In this, way children were supposed to solve problems that adults could not solve themselves. To Hannah Arendt desegregated schools were a disrespect of the child – Black or White! As she writes:

> *Children cannot be expected to handle them* [the conflicts] *and therefore should not be exposed to them.*
>
> (Arendt 1959: 55)

In the school, the child is not only exposed to but also expected to solve the problems of adult – and to do this in the arena of *the social* in which he is *"still a stranger, in which he cannot orient himself by his own judgment"* (ibid.).

> *To the extent that parents and teachers fail him as authorities, the child will conform more strongly to his own group, and under certain*

---

24 This is why *Reflections on Little Rock* now a day is read with great interest by advocates for gay marriages!

(Arendt 1959: 56)

Two aspects could be of interest in a Freedom Writer perspective:

First of all: The competencies to interact in *the social* do not come by naturally. They have to be learned – and taught. Without the authorities of parents and teachers, *the social* will in the hands of children turn into something evil and dystopian like in William Golding's *Lord of the Flies* and not into the utopian childhood province of freedom like in Astrid Lindgren's *Pippi Longstocking*. Gang-life comes due to failing adults ("adults" have nothing to do with age, but solely with attitude of responsibility) – due to the falling apart of *the private* and *the social*. Without guidance to navigate by, the children might easily develop anti-democratic and totalitarian tendencies – gangs, drug-run subcultures etc. When grown older they will not have the competences to take over and further develop the democratic societies. Understood in this way lack of adult responsibility and authority is a risk to both the children and the society! About the newspicture of Elizabeth Eckford being chased by the mob at Central High, Arendt writes:

The picture looked to me like a fantastic caricature of progressive education which, by abolishing the authority of adults, implicitly denies their responsibility for the world into which they have borne their children and refuses the duty of guiding them into it.

(Arendt 1959: 50)

130

Secondly, this perspective opens up the door for the responsible adult to step into character and become the needed guide. This guide can be a teacher like Erin Gruwell. Seen in the perspective of Hannah Arendt's *Reflections…* Ms. G, as she is called by her students, is bridging the triangle between *the private, the social* and *the political* by…

- …connecting her students with their individual *private* sphere through the narratives used in the diaries and thereby giving the student's lives a credit no one, even not the students themselves, had ever given them
- …connecting her students to each other in the realm of *the social* through her classroom leadership and the exercise work they undertook and thereby letting them develop acceptable rules of conduct in their interactions – acceptable rules to bring into a democratic society as grown-ups
- …connecting her students to the needs and demands of *the political* by teaching contents according to national standards and thereby educating them for a life in an open society.

On Revolution

Europeans are very fast to point fingers at Hollywood-films like *Freedom Writers* and categorize them as 'American' and thereby superficial and untrustworthy. This is one of the reasons why it might be a difficult job to introduce the methods in (northern) Europe. Why these differences between Europe and America?

In her book, *On Revolution* Arendt focuses on the similarities and differences between the American Revolutionary War from 1775 to 1783 and the French Revolution from 1789 to 1799. Both revolutions are expressed bourgeoisie showdown with societies of privileges, and both are based on thoughts and ideas of the Enlightenment – they stand along with Kant's words as seen above, as the final milestones of this Era.

The immediate difference lies in the importance of the social aspects. In France, the social destitution and misery was at that time obvious, and therefore very quickly became more important than democratic freedoms. Pity and commiseration became the emotions that controlled policy. These feelings, argues Arendt, are boundless and binds primarily to 'virtue of eloquence' and one's own degree of emotion. Moreover, pity leads to actions on the sufferer's behalf, which in Popper's Matrix is described as collective altruism. Most obvious are the social perspective of the revolutionary slogan (which are currently enrolled in the French Constitution) on *liberté*, *égalité* and *fraternité*, where the concept of freedom is negative – freedom from poverty – and where equality and fraternity as a definition of 'the good life' shows the binding of the nation to guarantee its citizens' happiness. In this way, the state gets ends of its own, and its citizens are forced to focus on *labor* in order to finance the state – and then we are back at the Plato-quotation from above: *...fitting people into a single unit, both using persuasion and power...*

The background of the American Revolution was quite different from the French. Misery was not on the agenda in America (at that time the misery of the slaves was not an issue!). The ability of the individual to make a living was higher than in Europe. The Americans had compassion for the actual Next, who inadvertently had ended up in poverty and traded in a specific, silent solidarity – in an individual altruism – with the individual. However, they never generalized the care aimed at a general misery.

Besides that, America had a democratic tradition that went back to 1620, to the Pilgrim Fathers on the Mayflower. Before the Pilgrims landed in New England, they signed the Mayflower Compact, in which…

> *…we solemnly and mutually in the presence of God and one another, Covenant and Combine ourselves together into a Civil Body Politic, for our better ordering and preservation and furtherance of the ends aforesaid; and by virtue hereof to enact, constitute and frame such just and equal Laws, Ordinance, Acts, Constitutions and Offices, from time to time, as shall be thought most meet and convenient for the general good of the Colony, unto which we promise all due submission and obedience.*
>
> (Bradford 1620)

The Pilgrim Covenant evolved into a council-based democracy in which villages, towns, districts and colonies could discuss and reach decisions on appropriate measures and conditions. This meant, among other things, that when the war of independence became a reality, it had strong support from the colonists' side – and they had very efficient lines of communication in a sparsely populated countryside.

This democratic tradition had taught Americans the joy of participation in public control, in *the politics*. It is this tradition that shines through in the words of the Declaration of Independence about the inalienable rights: *Life, Liberty and the Pursuit of Happiness*. The American concept of freedom is more ambiguous than the French, for as it of course has the negative meaning of freedom from absolute monarchial oppression, it also underlines to a high degree the positive freedom to act (including *action* in Arendt's understanding of the concept). And similar there is not in the American concept of *the pursuit of happiness* a commitment by the state to provide this happiness, such as the French slogan later put up to, only to create the framework for the individual's quest. Unfortunately, the wording *Pursuit of Happiness* is quite confusing as Jefferson's concept of happiness was centered around democratic participation, rather than on material gratification. That the wording became as it is, might be due perhaps to 'a fit of absent-mindedness' (Arendt 1963/2012: 289)! In this case, it is an absent-mindedness that because it was never explained and analyzed by the Americans themselves, can be blamed for the mass consuming 'American way of life' and for the Europeans general view of the American society as lacking solidarity and being ruled by extreme liberalists. And why in America today the focus too is on *labor* and not on neither *work* nor *action*! But that was, according to Arendt, never Jefferson's intentions.

As the two revolutions (ideally) is presented by Arendt they become archetypal for the two altruistic fields in Popper's Matrix, and as such they can say to have given significant contributions to the content dimension of the concept of *Bildung*. For both revolutions however, it applies that they initiate focus on what Arendt calls *labor*, i.e. household-economy, rather than *action* that is innovative, transformative and political. Focus is placed on the satisfaction of needs in the bottom of Maslow's pyramid. And when, after the fulfillment of the basic needs for food, clothing and shelter are satisfied, the societies have no more (read: Jefferson's democratic participation or Arendt's *ac-*

tion) to offer only further consumption is an option. This is perhaps the most important reason at all to seek a *Bildung* that promotes the individual altruism, the autonomous individual and the democratic participation – in the context of an Arendt-inspired pedagogy.

For the concept of humanity, the differences between the two revolutions' mindsets are huge. The French Revolution is based largely on Rousseau's philosophy, in which *God makes all things good; man meddles with them and they become evil* (Rousseau 1762/1974: 5). Only in the state of nature, man can be good. Any civilization creates degeneration and decay. Revolution, and thus pedagogy, must aim to restore the state of nature as much as possible. The ideology of equality and brotherhood is the essential idea for the realization of Rousseau's thoughts on centrally given happiness to the people (in the singular!). The people is thus at the mercy of external circumstances and has few or no opportunities to lift themselves out of poverty. Only the collective can promote the just material needs for satisfaction and happiness. But then the people are turned to the mercy of centralized power and do not have the autonomy-enhancing *Bildung*: Once government has embarked upon planning for the sake of justice, it cannot refuse the responsibility for anybody's fate or position.

The original human nature at Jefferson and "the Founding Fathers" is the exact opposite. It continues the tradition of the Pilgrim Fathers, who feared the state of nature (see Roderick Nash for a somewhat different interpretation of humanity and nature among the early settlers in America) they might expect in an only modestly civilized America. It was the civilized men's fear of the wild, and that this savagery could potentially make men into evil (selfish?) creatures. The medicine against the spoilage of wilderness was to make a binding covenant, creating a community where each through his acceptance of the pact remained within the framework of a controlling civilization. It is this binding community that is in focus in Arendt's concept of *action*, which is continued (or attempted reintroduced?) in the famous words from Kennedy's inaugural speech: *And so, my fellow Americans, ask not what your country can do for you, ask what you can do for your country* – a speech that greatly referred back to Jefferson and the Declaration of Independence. Men is thus primarily driven from within with a natural right (in U.S. rhetoric often 'given by God', see Pilgrim Covenant above and Kennedy's speech) to independently *act*. The American 'people' is a plural form, where the *actions'* steps and directions are not determined by external factors. The view of the human nature, which led to the American Revolution, is based on civilization, culture and authority in one's own life, including the altruistic obligation to help the concrete Other – in the best of Kantian understandings.

As the French Revolution progressed, the concept of 'consensus' and the will to dialogue were replaced with the concept of 'will' – 'will of the people', represented exclusively (in the strict sense of the word!) by Robespierre and the guillotine, opposite each individual's interests, and therefore also any economic system that might be based on such interests – which contributes to the prevailing 'capitalism anxiety' in our part of the world:

Thus is the 'common will'-articulation of a common interest, the people's or the nation's interest as a whole, and because of this interest or desire as common, its entire existence depends on that it stands in contrast to all individual interests and wills.

(Arendt 1963/2012: 74,
with a direct reference to
Rousseau's *The Social Contract*)

The American pluralistic understanding of 'people' and its practice of democratic participation in the sphere of *Action* regardless of rank or position is in sharp contrast to this.

The 'American way' is also illustrated in John Steinbeck's discussion of the Hebrew concept *timshel* in the novel *East of Eden*. In Genesis God uses the word *timshel* in a dialogue with Cain shortly before the fratricide. Normally the translation of *timshel* is either the imperative 'thou *shalt* rule over sin', subduing men in relation to God. Or the unavoidable 'thou *will* rule over sin', which also is a form of fatalism. Steinbeck instead suggest 'thou *mayest* rule over sin', which leaves men with the responsibility over their own lives. Because with a 'you can' there is also the possibility not to act. The individual decide for him or her self – in there lays the freedom of man.

In a more contemporary pedagogy the difference between the two revolutions are reflected in the European contra the American approaches to the above mentioned sentence *"he failed himself, his family, and you by choosing to be a victim of the environment"* (Gruwell 2009: 190). In Europe, it seems as if the starting point is the citizen's helplessness because of poor social conditions, and that the individual's responsibility is pushed much in the background. The result is 'pity', which legitimizes a massive intervention in 'benefit' of the citizen by the public. This position is in tune with the French Revolution's words about freedom from oppression and poverty and definition of happiness as based on equality and community. In the American view, you are basically responsible for your own choice of actions, and only in the second instance any responsibility can be reduced because of mitigating circumstances. This corresponds to the basic attitude of the words of The Declaration of Independence stating the right to seek happiness and freedom to act. In this field of tension between social responsibility and collective altruism on the one hand and on the other personal responsibility and individual altruism the education finds itself in an ethical dilemma: Is a 'good' life a human right which the state (school) must provide, or is it a human right, under orderly conditions, individually to seek happiness? Sharply put up the first one requires education for obedience to the common interest, while the second requires *Bildung* for courage to live!

Popper's Matrix may then be expanded with a few more signifiers [and personal conclusions]:

- The collective altruism: The European welfare systems. [Europe has a lack of individualism]
- The collective egoism: Some of America's (religious) militant groups (some even includes both white and black Americans), which precisely rejects high-society, but not their own small communities.
- The individual egoism: The lonely cowboy, emblem of the self-sufficient America under the Monroe Doctrine. [America has too much egoism]
- The individual altruism: Jefferson's ideal of happiness of democratic participation. [The ideal position where both America and Europe should meet!]

The general tone in both Freedom Writer books and the movie is to me the Jeffersonian (and with him Arendt and Popper) attitude, putting the emphasis on *'a sober combination of individualism and altruism'* (to use the words of Popper); to stress the responsibility of the individual *("choosing to be a victim of the environment"* and *"there are no excuses in life!")* combined with a strong will to help those in need – to give them courage to live.

In the movie this is seen for example in the scene, where Erin talks to André in the hall-way outside room 203. She scolds him for not showing up and for giving himself a bad self-evaluation. In addition, she says: *"I don't want excuses"*, meaning what she wants is responsibility. And at the same time she helps him: *"Pull yourself together, make a new evaluation – you are not going to fail!"*

Action and the critique of late modernity

In her probably most well-known book, *The Human Condition*, Hannah Arendt is contemplating over human life. To analyze it she is elaborating the three-fold division of activities (*Vita Activa*) also used in *Reflections on Little Rock*:

- *Labor* is the activity of sustaining human life. It is the double-sided activity of reproduction – producing food, eating and sleeping on the one hand and giving birth and raising children on the other. *Labor* is therefore the sphere of the family.
- *Work* is the activity of producing things not for direct consumption – things that will outlive its creator. The things produced by *work* distinguish humans from ani-

mals, and is what opens up the social world for the individual human being.

- *Action* is the human activity of the new, the innovative and the unforeseen. Within *action* concepts like forgiveness and promise is found, because the unforeseen unfortunately sometimes means that people are getting hurt. The human ability to start over again, to grant each other a second chance (so often an underlined idea in the world of the Freedom Writers!) is an act of forgiveness and very often followed by a promise to do better in the future. Where *labor* is individual (or at least taking place in *the private*) and *work* is the base for social life *action* demands such a social entity. *Action* is the sphere of politics – in a broad sense.

Hannah Arendt uses these three categories to raise a critique of the emerging mass societies of late modernity – the era that are fully unfolding itself in these years, more than 50 years after she wrote the book. Where the Jeffersonian 'freedom' focused on *work* and *action* in Hannah Arendt's analysis, the technical development and the ability of mass-production changed that focus towards *labor*. Mass consumption is exactly that: consumption also of the 'things' that within the realm of *work* should have lasted 'forever'. All foci are now on production for consume (often labelled as 'welfare') and for destruction in consume as the only way to fulfil 'the pursuit of happiness'. We have chosen materialism over democracy – maybe one of mankind's most important choices ever?

In my own country, Denmark, where the collective concepts from the French Revolution are still ruling the society, we no longer talk about a 'welfare society'. Instead, we have entered a 'society of competition'. Our government and its institutions, including all educational institutions, have only one goal; to squeeze as much power of labor (in the Marxian understanding of the word) out of the people in order to raise production, establishing an economy of growth and anaesthetize the population through even more consumption. A sedated population does not have to think, so in curricula all over the educational system aspects of *work*, *action* and even *Bildung* are disappearing. *Action* is substituted by behavior. Only *labor* is left. Once again, Plato can be quoted:

> *...fitting people into a single unit, both using persuasion and power. It lets them share any advantage that each individual can contribute to the community. And it's actually the law that creates people with the right attitude to the state, not to unleash them, so that everyone can go their own way, but to use them to weld together the city.*
>
> (Plato 2013: 98)

But a people without *work* and *action* – and without *Bildung* – are not forming a society. It is only a bunch of individuals living side by side, alienated from each other and not different from other living creatures. The people are losing its humanity. Men become *animal laborans*.

To those alienated who cannot find themselves a place in this 'society' criminality, gang-life and religious extremism seems to be an alternative. And neither the educational nor the social security systems have any tools available for this situation, because the tools – aspects of *work*, *action* and *Bildung* – are not 'efficient' in an economy of mass production and mass consumption! We have lost the toolbox.

But... within this grim description might be the seeds for a solution! The outstanding personalities of *Vita Activa* that I have known through-out my life – and among them are Erin Gruwell, founder of the Freedom Writers – all have *action* as their platform (not necessarily understood in the traditional political way), and run contrary to the mainstream ideology of the *labor*-enforcing 'society of competition'. They can teach us hope, by teaching with the heart to quote two of the Freedom Writers' book-titles.

For Hannah Arendt, as we saw above, the child will belong to the family and therefor to *labor*, whereas pedagogy and the school will transcend all three categories and actually form its own category. However, exactly then pedagogy is also able to draw on aspects of all three categories.

This is precisely what happens when the *Freedom Writers*-methodology uses the narrative approach and let participants write their stories. The three spheres of Hannah Arendt are transcended as the stories are based in *the private*, formulated and presented in the intersubjective realm of *the social*, and actually might have consequences for both the author, in order of self-identification and appreciation, and the readers – as a *political act*!

Narratives, like those produced along the ideas of the Freedom Writers, initiate new beginnings for the individual – and its surroundings. But more than that according to Hannah Arendt; narratives explore the meaning of the individual life, and media of this exploration is contemplation – thinking. Therefore the pedagogy of the Freedom Writers not only transcend the three spheres of *Vita Activa* it also include *Vita Contemplativa* – and therefore the 'whole human being'.

Understood in this way the Freedom Writers methodology is through forgiveness respecting and caring for the individual by giving it a second chance, a chance for a new beginning and a chance to become educated in the true meaning of the word – a writer of her or his own freedom!

Resources

- Arendt, Hannah (1958/1998): *The Human Condition*. University of Chicago Press, Chicago.

- Arendt, Hannah (1958/2005): *Menneskets vilkår*. Gyldendal, København.

- Arendt, Hannah (1959): Reflections on Little Rock. IN *Dissent*, 53: 45-56.

- Arendt, Hannah (1963/2006): *Eichmann in Jerusalem*. Penguin Classics, New York.

- Arendt, Hannah (1963/2012): *Om Revolution* [On Revolution]. Klim, Aarhus.

- Bradford, William (1620): The Mayflower Compact. IN Bradley et.al.: *The American Tradition on Literature*, 1. Grosset and Dunlap, New York.

- Gruwell, Erin (ed.)(2009): *Teaching Hope*. Broadway Books, New York.

- Kant, Immanuel (1784): *Beantwortung der frage: Was ist aufklärung?* [What is Enlightenment?]. Berlinische Monatsschrift. Dezember-Heft.

- Korsgaard, Morten Timmermann (2014): *Hannah Arendt og pædagogikken. Fragmenter til en gryende pædagogik* [Hannah Arendt and the pedagogics. Fragments of a dawning pedagogic]. Aarhus Universitetsforlag, Aarhus.

- Løgstrup, K.E. (1986): *Den etiske fordring* [The Ethical Demand]. Gyldendal, Copenhagen.

- Nash, Roderick (1967/1973): *Wilderness and the American Mind.* Yale University Press, Hew Haven.

- Petersen, Arne Friemuth (1985): *Toward a Rational Theory of the Mind: Lifelines in Popper's Deductive Approach to Psychology.* ETC #42, vol. 3.

- Petersen, Michael Bang (2012): *Social Welfare as Small-Scale Help: Evolutionary Psychology and the Deservingness Heuristic.* American Journal of Political Science, Vol. 56, Nr. 1.

- Platon (2013): *Staten. Samlede værker IV* [Republic. Collected works IV]. Gyldendal, Copenhagen.

- Platon (2014): *Lovene. Samlede værker V* [Laws. Collected works V]. Gyldendal, Copenhagen.

- Popper, Karl (1945/1973): *The Open Society and Its Enemies, Vol. I and II.* Routledge, London.

- Popper, Karl (1979): *Objective Knowledge.* Clarendon Press, Oxford.

- Popper, Karl (1989): *Conjectures and Refutations.* Routledge, London.

- Rousseau, Jean-Jacques (1762/1974): *Émile.* Everyman's Library, London.

- Ydegaard, Torbjørn (2013): *Kritisk-rationel pædagogik* [Critical-rational pedagogy]. Books on Demand, Copenhagen.

About the author

Torbjørn Ydegaard is Danish but educated as mentor of outdoor life from The Norwegian School of Mountaineering and hold a Master of Education from University of Oslo, Norway. He is also educated Freedom Writer Teacher. Torbjørn is currently teaching pedagogy at University College South-Denmark. His students range from bachelors of Nutrition and Health to soldiers in the armed forces. Besides that Torbjørn is Chairman of the Board in the Danish NGO Himalayan Project that runs among other things school empowerment projects in a mountain region in Nepal. Contact: tyde@ucsyd.dk.

The Freedom Writers

Freedom Writers Foundation
PO BOX 41505
Long Beach, CA 90852
www.freedomwritersfoundation.org

Books etc.

- Garrett, Darrius (2013): *Diary of a Freedom Writer. The Experience.* Tate Publishing, Mustang, OK.

- Gruwell, Erin (1999): *The Freedom Writers Diary.* Broadway Books, New York.

- Gruwell, Erin (2007a): *The Freedoms Writers Diary. Teacher's Guide.* Broadway Books, New York.

- Gruwell, Erin (2007b): *Teach With Your Heart.* Broadway Books, New York.

- Gruwell, Erin (2009): *Teaching Hope.* Broadway Books, New York.

- Hurwin, Davida Wills (2009): *Freaks and Revelations.* Little, Brown and Company, New York.

- Knüfken, Jörg (2013): *Das Wunder Bleibt Aus.* CareLine, Stamsried.

- LaGravanese, Richard (dir.)(2007): *Freedom Writers.* Paramount Pictures.

- Omaha Young Writers Project (2011): *In my Shoes. Teen Reflections on Hope & the Future.* WriteLife, Omaha NE.

- Schober, Anne (2014): *Heart Prints.* Library Tales Publishing, New York.
- Ydegaard, Torbjørn (2014b): *Everybody Has a Story. Erasmus 2014.* Books on Demand, Copenhagen.

FSC
www.fsc.org
MIX
Papir fra
ansvarlige kilder
Paper from
responsible sources
FSC® C105338